school
of
wishing

Praise for *School of Wishing*

"The correlation between my teachings and this new book are profoundly significant. When I was asked to review *School of Wishing*, I was delighted to support the notion that sending out a wish to the Universe can have such positive and life-changing outcomes. Brainard and Delia have written a thought-provoking book that doesn't just provide answers but makes you think about your own values and the life journey you're on, but more importantly how a simple wish can influence and have such a lasting effect."

—John Holland, Psychic Medium & Spiritual Teacher, author of *Born Knowing* **and** *The Spirit Whisperer*

"Brainard and Delia Carey have written a powerful book on the complex nature of wishing and have not provided an easy answer, but a *contemplative look* at why and how wishing works."

—Christine Hassler, author of *20-Something, 20-Everything* **and the** *20 Something Manifesto*

"Brainard and Delia Carey have written the definitive manual on how best to have your wishes fulfilled. They've made my wishful thinking come true!"

—Ellen Whitehurst, bestselling author of *Make This Your Lucky Day*, **coach and speaker**

school of wishing

Lessons to Change Your Life and Make Your Dreams Come True

Brainard and Delia Carey

Skyhorse Publishing

Skyhorse Publishing books may be purchased in bulk at
special discounts for sales promotion, corporate gifts,
fund-raising, or educational purposes. Special editions
can also be created to specifications. For details, contact
the Special Sales Department, Skyhorse Publishing,
307 West 36th Street, 11th Floor, New York, NY 10018 or
info@skyhorsepublishing.com.

Skyhorse® and Skyhorse Publishing® are registered
trademarks of Skyhorse Publishing, Inc.®, a Delaware
corporation.

Visit our website at www.skyhorsepublishing.com.

10 9 8 7 6 5 4 3 2 1

Library of Congress Cataloging-in-Publication Data is
available on file.

ISBN: 978-1-62636-115-7

Printed in China

CONTENTS

Part ①

Course Materials for Part 2: The School of Wishing

1. This book.

2. Optional smartphone or computer and an understanding of the term "hashtag."

3. An open mind.

4. A desire for even one great wish to come true.

5. The authors' website to get your free diploma, www.schoolofwishing.com.

6. A frame to hang your diploma!

Reading Materials

The Ingenious Gentleman Don Quixote of La Mancha, by Miguel de Cervantes

The Interpretation of Dreams, by Sigmund Freud

I Am That, by Nisargadatta Maharaj

A Course in Miracles, by the Foundation for Inner Peace

Autobiography of a Yogi, by Paramahansa Yogananda

Tao Te Ching, by Lao Tzu and Stephen Mitchell

The Bible (Jerusalem Bible or other edition)

Give and Take: A Revolutionary Approach to Success, by Adam
M. Grant, PhD

Acknowledgments

THIS BOOK WAS not written by a single author, it was written by you and the collective wishers and dreamers out there who would like to tap into the wisdom of old philosophers and new ones, to see more wishes come true, to see a life touched by magic, a life that is full of promise and possibility because it has the foundation of knowledge.

This has been published because there is a constant thirst for a different angle that reawakens us to the essential tools of our life and our mind. This book is one new angle, one new voice that may ignite a familiar spark already within you. It was also written by us, Brainard and Delia Carey, a couple who have been practicing the philosophy of wishing with success and failure, because we all have an ideal life or a desire for change that we would like to see come true. Who doesn't wish for something?

We must acknowledge the great philosophers who are the basis of so much of the wisdom we are all distilling in different forms.

So many people made this book possible, including the publisher and agent we have. It was edited by Thornwell May, to whom we are indebted. Tad Crawford is also a person who has become a good friend and without him, this book would not have been made at all, because he encouraged the publisher to take it on.

Richard Bolger is our very close friend who took all the images for this book, and without him this would not be nearly as beautiful. We are grateful to him for his contribution. The images are meant for you to gaze upon and extract information from, in the same way you do with great paintings. All the images were chosen because of a certain quality they have, the ability to communicate a visual experience that transcends, or points to, who we are or who we could be, on a daily basis, even for just a moment—they are windows into a separate reality that can contribute to this one.

Introduction

"**I WISH I** had a wish to wish a wish away"—Donovan

This book was written to change our lives and yours. It is a book that has the loftiest possible goal, which is to help your wishes and your dreams come true. It is called the *School of Wishing* because this is also about creating a community of support for everyone who would like to attend a free school of wishing. If you read no further, send a wish out into the world and hashtag it on Twitter, Vine, or some other platform, and you will find others who have the same hopeful vibe and outlook supporting your thought.

The format is: [Your wish here]#schoolofwishing

See you in the ether, the Internet, or the virtual worldwide net of communication! At the least, the Internet is a system of thoughts, so why not add positively to the mass of ideas out there? We are told to be "careful what we wish for," and the reason is that wishes that are verbalized and written down have a tendency to come true.

We all have a sense of justice and of intelligent discrimination, and of course we all desire love and a measure of success in life in general. We are all searching for meaning and for new ways to have a consistent, fulfilling experience in life, and this book is a guide to that process of arriving at your own philosophy, your own way to navigate your wishes using your mind—to investigate, evaluate, and develop a strategy for yourself.

Above our bed we have a small work of art we made, which is a hand-embroidered canvas that says, "Our dreams will come true." That has been up there for almost seven years now, and it is a constant reminder that we are searching, waiting, and hoping for a dream to become reality. This book is one of those dreams. The steps to get here were specific.

We take this seriously, and have witnessed the possibilities and the real fruits of wishing, which includes the publication of this book. This is also a course that is meant to stimulate your own contemplation of what it means to have more resources available for you to make those ideas come true. This book contains an online element that is a classroom that you can be a part of at www.schoolofwishing.com. If you complete this course section that begins on chapter 7, we will send you a certificate that is a diploma in wishing, giving you the groundwork necessary so that you can teach and share this process if you want to, thus strengthening your own power and convictions.

You can teach wishing by sharing the course in the second half of this book with any group that you form.

Ancient Civilizations

When we think about wishing, it carries the weight of ancient civilizations who conjured up genies in bottles and granted three life-changing wishes. In early stories from fairy tales, we know that sometimes getting everything you want can be problematic, and having that one last wish to undo your previous wish is the most important one of all in some cases. "Be careful of what you wish" implies that what you wish for might come true no matter how casually you wished it, and that you have to take some responsibility for it. If that statement holds any truth, it asks the question: how do we take responsibility for that, and how can we be more careful to end up with what we truly want if it is happening by default otherwise?

The Search for Meaning

We are living in a time where there are many books on how to succeed with something close to wishing. Terms like "aligning yourself with the universe" or getting into the "vortex" or learning the "secret" are ways in which we are told that we can get many of the things we want. What do we really want? When you make a wish, perhaps on your birthday, do you wish for material gain, or perhaps world peace? Our lives in many ways are based on our ability to wish for and nurture what it is we desire, and perhaps that is even the meaning of life itself.

Victor Frankl wrote a book called *Man's Search for Meaning*, and in it he describes a type of therapy he developed which had its genesis when he was in a concentration camp for Jews in Germany in World War II. As a Jew in a concentration camp, he was essentially being worked to death. He describes marching in the snow, in clothing about as protective as pajamas. Though he feared dying, he also had another thought process: he was wondering why so many prisoners didn't have a common cold in these harsh conditions. What was keeping them alive against all odds? For himself, he felt that there was something in him that was keeping him alive, a particular goal he had. That goal was to write a book. He thought to himself that if he could survive this situation, he would write a book. In fact, with all his heart he wanted to survive so that he could complete the goal of writing a book that was in part about the concentration camp experience. He was trained as a psychologist, and though he was in an extreme situation and being slowly killed, he was thinking that if he could only live through it, he would write a book.

The mind is a curious organ with abilities to overcome situations that are neither rational nor understandable. Victor

Frankl did survive, through luck, and perhaps his will was an element, and he wrote books and also created a type of therapy he dubbed "logotherapy." When a client would come to him as a psychologist because of depression or a difficult situation, Frankl would ask a startling question. He would say to them that if things were really so bad, then why didn't they kill themselves? This of course was very disturbing to the client who would balk at that suggestion and ask what he was talking about.

Frankl would go on to explain that if the situation was really so bad, if things were that awful, why not end your life and be free of the pain? Again the client was horrified at the suggestion. So Frankl would gently ask what it was that they were living for. In other words, when the pain of life gets almost too difficult to bear, what is it, he was asking, that keeps us going? He felt that there was an answer that was specific to everyone. For Frankl, the answer was to write books and work with clients developing his therapy. His clients said a range of things, like "I want to see my kids grow up and go to college." Or perhaps, "I want to take the trip to Alaska I have been saving for all these years!"

Then Frankl would say that if you want to see your kids grow up, and that is why you are not ending your life to escape from challenges and perhaps depression, then your kids, for now, represent the meaning of your life. If it is that trip to Alaska, to see the Aurora Borealis, then that is the meaning of your life. It takes an admission of feeling sad, disappointed, or depressed with your current situation to begin this thinking.

What Would You Miss the Most?

It is provocative and, for some, an impossible idea to determine the meaning of life for an individual, but the approach Frankl is taking allows us all to access that. If you knew your life was going to end soon, what is it that you would miss the most?

Frankl was being marched to death in a concentration camp, and he had a wish. That wish was to survive in order to write his book. His wish was also fulfilled, but why?

Perhaps it was in part because he was a young man during the time he was in the concentration camp, but many young people also died. It is hard to say exactly why he survived; luck was a big part, but he attributes it in part to his thought process, and he felt that he was not alone. He observed that his fellow camp mates were also surviving against the odds, and it was because life itself was clearly in the balance. It was not a matter of just getting through the day and battling life's difficulties and relationships—it was life or death. Under extreme circumstances, which hopefully none of us will ever have to endure, the mind must make a decision, and there must be a place, a resource within, from which to pull so that you can have or even see the possibility of survival. That resource may be God as an external form, or God as in your Self, that is perhaps powerful enough, omnipotent even, to overcome extremes. It is perhaps, the essence of hope.

Inner Resources

We will focus on how we identify and use our inner resources for the purpose of this book. Because if we can see the meaning of our own lives in terms of goals that are driving us to live, then we will understand more about the way wishing works. The messages that we receive from various pop culture books will also be examined, because as ancient as the wish is, so are the charlatans and snake oil salesmen who promote miracles and cures from as far back as medieval Europe to today. We will look at philosophers and historic examples of solid thinking that seem to aid us in understanding ourselves and our own intellectual powers.

It is the humble wish of these authors that this book is taken for what it is, an examination of the process of what seems to work and what does not in the realm of improving your lot through wishing. We read philosophy and also, we are readers of many pop books on the subject of miracles and wishes, and will offer our analysis on why some contemporary books and techniques seem to work, while others do not.

The images shown here are all taken by Richard Bolger, and just as the text seeks to uncover the process of how we wish, the images are a manifestation of how an artist sees the world as a magical place, a place of possibility. How is it that the ordinary images we see daily can be turned into something almost miraculous when viewed by the eyes of an artist in a poetic way? The images are designed to use the part of your brain that these words will not reach, the part that is still dreaming of another way, another place, another life, a different but not separate reality. Gaze at the images. There are mysteries in each to uncover.

How To Use This Book

This book begins with six chapters of reading and part 2 contains the course.

The course is designed to enable critical thinking while also striving for a true shift in consciousness. There are three ways of completing this course.

1. Acquire the books that are assigned reading, and read what you can of each book on the day required and add to the blog on each day to receive a diploma. With this method, the course will last for eleven days.

2. Acquire the books, then on the day required to read them, stretch that day of the course into a week to get deeper into the texts, which are designed to change your mind in a profound and meaningful way. The course will take eleven weeks this way. You can contribute to the blog and receive your diploma when you are done.

3. Skip the required reading altogether, do not acquire the books, but read the eleven daily exercises of breathing and

wishing upon waking up and going to sleep each day. Add to the blog on each day of the exercises and receive your diploma.

This is not a simple or easy course to complete. It is designed to generate new thinking and to retrain your mind to achieve things you never thought possible. For some it can happen quickly while others must work harder. As authors and teachers we are accessible through the blog to help you.

Imagine how good it will feel to finish the course and have a new perspective on making your wishes come true, in the context of a thoughtful and critical approach to the literature and ideas discussed.

CHAPTER 1

How We Wished This Book into Existence

WE HAVE BEEN artists since before we met, and like so many artists, had a variety of dreams. One of them was getting into a big New York art show like the Whitney Museum Biennial which we did, and if you are interested in learning about how that happened, you can read it in our previous book, *The Art of Hugging*. Another dream we had was writing books to share with the whole world about health and spirituality—motivational books that will bring happiness to the people who read them as well as facts and questions with a sense of hope that can change the reader's life in some form. We kept working on different book proposals while juggling ideas back and forth between ourselves. We really wanted our first book to be successful.

When artists talk like this to family and friends they are summarily written off because the approach is usually all enthusiasm without an understanding of follow through. We also had no trust fund, no regular job, and were gambling on a lifestyle without stability every day and the stakes got higher with the birth of our child in 2001, two years after we met. This book we are writing right now is the fourth one. We were in the Whitney Biennial and almost everything we wished for has come true. Why? Perhaps it was a combination of our desires coupled with plenty of hard work, tears, difficult lessons, and setbacks. Our good fortune was also fueled by the love we have for one another, because without that, it is hard to go on after failure, after rejection, or other forms of not getting what you want, when you want it.

We all need support, especially when we feel there is little hope, or that time has passed us by.

The Dream of Writing a Bestseller

The story of how we got to the improbable place of having an agent and a publisher is a telling one. Ever since we met and began brainstorming together about how we were going to make money and avoid getting a traditional job, the classic idea of writing a bestseller kept popping up into our heads. We started gathering books from the library that described how to write books and find an agent, all of which cautioned against any quick fix approach to the daunting world of publishing. And this was while we were heading into one of the worst economic depressions in recent times.

Friends Who Became Millionaires

There was one bit of personal history that kept us moving along, and that was the childhood story of Brainard, coauthor of this book, and his parents' friends who decided to write a bestseller to make money, and actually did just that with an appearance on *Oprah* to seal the deal. It was a powerful lesson because Brainard's parents were teachers and musicians, and their friends were teachers as well, not entrepreneurs. The conversation around the dinner table and at gatherings was more likely to be songs that were sung, or what was being taught at a school, than anything about making money or entrepreneurial ideas. Then one of his parents' friends got divorced, and remarried, and suddenly the conversation from this newly formed couple was all about their book their new diet book. They chose to write a diet book, because they felt that would be the idea that would bring them the most money. They did in fact make bundles of money in a short period of time from their book. They also became more and more estranged from their friends. As a college student at the time, Brainard was watching this all happen. Admittedly, they talked so much about their book that they became a bit boring. But what was even worse was that they kept encouraging everyone else to write a book. This eventually drove a wedge between all their relationships, and stunningly, they eventually left and moved to Disney World where they live today. It was a success story that is not unusual in that they were part of a community of middle class teachers and musicians, and suddenly they became rich and were following their dream—talking about money and books with a great passion all the time and alienating their friends, who often made fun of them in their absence and argued with them about their behavior when they were around. Relatives still reminisce about the successful couple, jokingly telling everyone over dinner, "You could write a book, anyone can!" What is clear to us now, that we couldn't appreciate back then, is that whenever you have a passion, and a strong belief, it increases the odds of getting what you want. It also can increase tension between friends who do not appreciate your ambitions because they lack those ambitions and find that your success challenges their professional success.

Travels to the Magic Kingdom

Now flash forward ten years, Brainard is married and has a child with his wife Delia (the coauthor of this book), and as he is singing songs to his child at bedtime, he remembers the authors of the diet book. Thinking fondly of the songs they used to all sing together, which he was now singing, he wrote the diet-book author an email, thanking him for the songs they used to sing (which Brainard still had a photocopy of, made by the authors of that diet book).

After Brainard wrote to the authors (yes, living in Disney World), they responded quickly and invited the whole family to Disney for an all-expenses-paid trip for four days. Those authors had continued to write books and were still millionaires. We decided to go because we had never been to Disney World, and now we also wanted to talk to them about how they got their book published as well as managed to have a great time. As adults, we had a different perspective on what these authors had done and had renewed respect for them as people choosing their own path and breaking ranks with everyone around them because of it. As we all grow up and have children or not, life teaches us lessons that we previously could not have understood.

So we flew down to Florida and got an unusual insight into how these authors managed the world around them with great savvy and manipulation, to our endless amazement. This is what happened.

Life in Disney World

They were living like ecstatic hermits in a way. They shunned most friends, didn't communicate with their families, and were otherwise very positive and enthusiastic, and very generous with us. Since they lived at Disney World, they knew the place as well as you would know your hometown neighborhood. Most people wait in long lines at Disney or buy expensive passes to get to the front of some lines. They had a pass that got them instantly to the front of every line. The pass was for people like celebrities to avoid getting mobbed, but of course they were not those kind of celebrities. But it gets better. They knew everyone as you would if you were the mayor of your hometown. That is, a very popular mayor in a tiny town.

At every single ride we were about to board, one of the authors would say to the person handling the lines something like this, "Disney is a special place, but like a theatre, there is no magic without the performers like you, and we want to say thanks by giving you this button, for bringing the magic here."

It is easy to remember that line because we heard it hundreds of times. They handed out personalized buttons all day to people working on the rides. The buttons were about two inches wide and had the authors' pictures on them as well as the phrase "We Appreciate You." Who wouldn't want a button like that? The result was that when we were on a roller coaster ride like Space Mountain, we could hear shouts of greetings from the roller coaster controllers over the loud speakers to our friends. They had the whole world of Disney loving them. At the end of a ride like Space Mountain, the operators would ask us to come into the control room for fun, or even ask if we wanted to stay on the ride for another round! Anyone who has been to Disney World in Florida knows this is not the typical experience there. We never, ever, waited on any line.

Lunch Conversation about Publishing

As we were having lunch we asked them more about books and how their careers developed while they were looking for an agent to get their book published. We had to read between the lines of what they were telling us because we knew that they were more shrewd than they let on. Their story is that they wrote a book containing ten different diets, made more than a dozen physical copies, and brought it in person to publishing houses in New York, delivering it by hand. A publisher picked it up and gave them a contract. They were also advised to use a "packager," which is a person or team of people who edit the book in such a way that it will have a mass-market appeal. Then, as the writers' dream goes, they were asked to be on *Oprah*, and that made them millionaires.

We told them about book ideas we had and asked them for tips on how to approach an agent or a publisher. They told us to describe to the publisher where our book would sit on the shelf of a bookstore, that is, between which titles. They didn't give us much more information that helped, but what did inspire us was watching them work the entirety of Disney World. These

authors were able to bend the world around them (quite literally) to their desires. What they wanted at Disney World was to be treated like royalty. They were, and this is the story of why.

Giving Away to Receive

They gave away buttons to everyone that worked there. Their buttons said that the recipient of the button was a wonderful person and it had a picture of the authors and their website on there. It was promotional genius. But it was more than that, because they were not trying to promote their books, they were promoting themselves. Everyone loved them and laid out the red carpet for them, because they had given almost every employee of Disney World a button to wear and collect, telling them how wonderful they were. They were the mascots of the Disney parade one year, and everywhere we went it was if we were with celebrities. But the only thing about them that anyone recognized was not that they were authors but that they were the people who went around complimenting everyone. They are a success story and the way they conduct their lives is indicative of that. They got just what they wished for. They were millionaires living in Disney World! Often, when we tell this story to friends, it seems incredulous and offen-

sive to some of them, but step back and look at the structure of
what they did. There is a lesson to be learned in marketing on
a grassroots level.

Our Plan in Action

Now we flash forward a few years, and we are two artists still
trying to write a book, with a ten-year-old child whom we are
home schooling. We are driven. We are reading books like *The
Secret*, and other self-help and positive thinking books, some of
which we thought would work, but later realized what was missing from all of them—the details, and intelligent wisdom. That
will be discussed in the next chapter.

As artists, we were continuing to exhibit our work, and
since we have had a successful career as conceptual artists in
New York and around the globe, other artists kept asking us how
we got into these shows, and how were we able to be such successful artists? Our first exhibit together was giving out hugs
and foot-washings to the public. That may not sound like art to
many people, but it was art when we got into prestigious shows
like the Whitney Museum Biennial doing it. However, we still
wanted to write that bestseller to fund the growing costs of living in New York City as well as to share all the love and passion
we had for different subjects.

The next thing we did was to write a newsletter to help
all the artists who were asking us about how we got into major

museum shows. Brainard was also consulting with artists on building strategies for how to get an exhibit at a gallery or a museum, because artists wanted more than our story, they wanted to know how to craft letters and applications too: the details. Then a real miracle happened. A publisher wrote one day and asked if we wanted to write a book for artists. At first we thought it was one of those offers where you have to pay to be in a who's who book, so we wrote back that we wanted a meeting right away. Sure enough, he was real, with an office in New York City and within a month we had a contract and a small advance check for our first book, titled *Making It in the Art World*.

The Lesson of Compliments and Hugs

Did wishing get us that contract? In the sense that our wish to write a book had spurred us to try all kinds of tactics, yes it did. But can we say it was definitively our wishing that did it? As much as Victor Frankl can say he survived because he wanted to write a book, we were trying hard for years to write and then suddenly it happened. At that moment, it was part of the meaning of our lives that was coming to fruition. We were searching everywhere and finally found what we were after, but it came to us in a way we never expected. Nevertheless, it was what we were wishing for, and it came true. The evidence is in your hands right now.

The reason for telling the story of the authors in Disney World—giving out buttons and becoming popular in that strange, insular world—and for telling our own story of artistic success in New York City—is to highlight a single common thread. By giving away compliments or their symbolic equivalent (we gave out hugs and foot-washings, while they gave out buttons), people were generally attracted to those activities, and when you are surrounded by people who wish you well, it seems good things tend to happen. Certainly it is better than the opposite and it is something we can control and perhaps manipulate within reason. The authors living in Disney World were attracting a ton of fans by reaching out to them one by one, with a clear strategy.

If we are more giving in nature, instead of asking all the time, the odds begin to increase that we will get what we are after, if for no other reason than we have more real friends who would like to help us in some way, because they feel they have been helped. It is a natural human reaction to want to return a favor, especially a compliment or gesture of comfort.

We are drawing a logical conclusion here based on our experience, but what if that does not make sense, yet is real to many? Like a miracle? We may have wished this book into existence along with hard work, but there was a surprise call we didn't predict. So, sudden and unexpected ways of achieving success may also have something to do with wishing for it.

Miracle Healing

If we look at Lourdes, France, the site of numerous healing miracles, it might give us another reason to think about what it is that constitutes a true miracle.

In the process of sanctifying an individual, the Vatican must research and validate the miracles that the saint-in-the-making is said to have performed. Of the thousands of people who go to Lourdes every year, claiming to have experienced a miracle, only sixty-seven are confirmed. Bernadette Soubirous witnessed apparitions in Lourdes in the nineteenth century, and as reports of miraculous healings spread, the papal investigations began. These are the same investigations the Vatican does today to decide if someone should become a saint or not. It is done with formality and rigor. Like any investigation, people are interviewed and local authorities are consulted. In the case of the Vatican, there is also a person whose job it is to suggest other possible reasons for the inexplicable, a devil's advocate, so to speak. Perhaps the sick person was not that sick, or that bone was not really broken, and so on. Like any investigation, the first thing that needs to be resolved is error or misrepresentation. Most cases similar to that of Bernadette Soubirous in Lourdes are declared invalid. This is important because it means a miracle (which we will discuss more later) is something that must either be proven, or that the circumstances surrounding a possible miracle must be without holes, with no room for foul play or outright lies. We rely on these basic ideas when investigating a crime, so why shouldn't the same criteria be used for proving the validity of a miracle?

In the next chapter we are discussing the roles of the books we were reading, how they played into our process of writing this book and achieving other dreams. Also we discuss what we have learned about the details of some authors' success, how they stepped into that success, which they claimed anyone could have done.

CHAPTER 2

New Age Gurus and Missing Pieces

THE INFAMOUS BOOK called *The Secret*, by Rhonda Byrne, first started as an Internet-only video. In a brilliant piece of marketing, the video had a great trailer, and for four dollars you could stream the video on your computer at a time when even Netflix wasn't streaming videos. *The Secret* video promised to reveal an answer to the unsolved question of how to succeed and get more of everything that you wish for. It would reveal the "ancient secret." The very same secret Beethoven presumably used, and countless others who were now dead, like master inventors and writers. The director of that video was Rhonda Byrne, a former television producer who had investors behind her to produce the campaign that was incredibly successful, making her a self-made millionaire. We were watching that video at the time, and in essence it tells you that if you wish hard enough and "align yourself with the universe" you will "attract" what you want. It was a compelling presentation, though low budget, and it provided us with a modern day Alladin's lamp—with the right instructions you could conjure the genie that would grant your wishes. It was nearly spelled out exactly like that, complete with genie images and contemporary self-help authors claiming they used the "secret" and all of their goals (mostly goals of material success) came true.

Multimillion Dollar Success

The interesting part of the video is how it was produced and how it became a multimillion dollar phenomena. Initially the video was narrated by Esther Hicks, a new age guru who channels a voice she calls "Abraham" and writes books and travels the world giving lectures. Esther Hicks talks about "attracting" the things you want by getting into alignment with the universe. She was talking about that for decades before Rhonda Byrne, and was tapping into early twentieth-century literature like Charles Haanel's *Master Key System* from 1912, Prentice Mulford's nineteenth-century *Thoughts Are Things*, Robert Collier's *Secret of the Ages*, from 1926, Napoleon Hill's bestselling book *Think and Grow Rich*, in 1937, and Norman Vincent Peale's *Power of Positive Thinking*, in 1952.

These are all "prosperity consciousness" books, and perhaps the most recent versions are books like Malcolm Gladwell's *Blink* and other works of his that outline various recipes for how to achieve success. Gladwell presented the idea that after ten thousand hours of work on something you become a master. There are no real studies to prove that, but it sounds good and is often accepted as fact, which it certainly is not. He uses cases to support his theories like the Beatles playing ten thousand hours before they came to America, while ignoring the countless musicians and artists throughout history who have toiled away for the same amount of time or more and received no accolades for being a master of their craft. He doesn't try to explain that, because it doesn't fit his theory, and like so many preachers on the recipes of success, anything that contradicts the author's ideas is ignored in most cases. It is too bad more authors don't challenge themselves to find the truth, or what points to the truth, rather than using an airtight marketing system designed to enrich them. Both are possible and why not embrace the dualities that often conflict? We want everything and nothing—material wealth and spiritual minimalism.

This is the world of books in the self-help genre, of a particularly positivistic style, and this book too fits in there, although we are looking at different systems as well as proposing one, which is the course presented in this book. Most authors have areas that they intentionally overlook to make their case. We also may be overlooking areas, but we are doing our best not to.

Esther Hicks

Esther Hicks is and was very popular and has written numerous books on the idea of "attracting wealth." In the first video of *The Secret*, Esther Hicks narrates almost the entire video and gives the video its basic argument and content, which is to say that we must use our minds to get what we want and that process is one you can train yourself to do. And, if after doing that, you do not get what you want, then it is because you are not in "alignment with the universe." Before we talk about what "alignment" is or is not, let's look at how the producer of *The Secret* attracted millions of dollars.

After the online video of *The Secret* became a big seller, Rhonda Byrne, who was partnering with Esther Hicks, decided to remove her image from it altogether. Initially Hicks had the right to approve the film's final cut. When she began voicing objections, Byrne began getting other actors for the voice-over to replace Esther Hicks. Instead of the larger percentage Hicks was promised, Byrne said she was cutting her percentage to almost nothing and restructuring the film into something different. This was devastating to Hicks who put a lot of time into the production, and she felt betrayed, and so there was only one answer she could give Byrne and that was her reluctant withdrawal from the deal. Byrne took her out of the video and replaced the entire narrative that Hicks had set up with a very similar one. The video went on to great success with an appearance on *Oprah* and a book of the same name followed. Esther Hicks was so furious that even though she claimed she didn't need the money or the fame, she literally lost her voice for a period of time. She could not speak in public at first, and when she did, she talked about how tremendously upset she was at Byrne and her tactics, while also trying to be as positive as possible and saying she didn't need the money anyway.

Savvy Capitalists

The reason we are explaining all this is because Rhonda Byrne did not simply "attract" success, she was a shrewd and perhaps cut-throat entrepreneur. In a capitalist society we support such tactics; we encourage them, in fact.

The savviest capitalist will rise at the expense of others, in almost all cases, because the goal for most entrepreneurs is not to help or generate community. It is simply to generate money for themselves. *The Secret* is an example of great marketing and a terrific New Age scandal because the workings of the main director were simply those of any aggressive entrepreneur who left a wake of betrayal in her brilliant path to success. Though articles were written about this conflict in the *New York Times* and other papers, it did not attract nearly as much attention as the multimillion dollar campaign Byrne continued to run on behalf of her project. The several people she interviewed on her video were also very savvy writers, entrepreneurs who have reputations of doing whatever it takes to get to the top, including Jack Canfield, who talks about embracing the *National Enquirer* as a means to promote his new book, along with other marketing and partnership deals.

So the truly deceptive notion of *The Secret* is that getting what you want is about wishing and hoping only, and that is the secret. The hard work and savvy entrepreneurial effort is left out, and that is how the public likes it. In the end you are left hungry and perhaps starving for more information because there are missing pieces and you are left to feel that you are just not doing it right somehow.

This is how the mass of people are led astray, by hearing the words we desire most, "your wish will come true if you just believe..." when in fact it takes a good dose of business sense and careful follow through, as well as a good title, like *The Secret*.

Aligning Yourself with the Universe?

This is a deeply misunderstood term that deserves some examination because it was the last fundamental step to getting what you want in Byrnes's video and book. Other authors also talk about this process of aligning yourself, especially all the authors just mentioned, in what is known as "prosperity consciousness." Though it is a bit vague, it means that you have to feel at peace with what you want. So if you want a million dollars, you have to feel you deserve it and that it will come to you. If you don't get it, the reasoning goes, it is because you are not aligning yourself correctly. Examples are given of being in alignment that you might recognize, such as, do you ever have a day where everything is going well and you find that synchronicity is everywhere? That is an example of being in alignment, but how to achieve that and turn it on at will is elusive. We know it when it happens, and it feels almost magical, but how to harness that? In the case of the authors who have made a living off of that, it is the work of selling their books and videos to the public that is hardball entrepreneurship, and that part is always left out of the equation when explaining the process. Another popular phrase that sums it up is "Success is ninety-nine percent per-spiration and one percent inspiration." We would like it to be the opposite, but hard work and strong focus are the tired words that make much of that happen. There are other elements, but the hard work cannot be avoided in almost all cases.

In the case of Victor Frankl, it is not so much about being an entrepreneur as it is taking the time to think about what your life really needs and what that means to you. He did want to write a book, and had to go through the process of getting his book published, and while there is a bit of presentation finesse needed for that, he was by no means an aggressive marketer. He was a purveyor of ideas that he used during his therapeutic sessions with clients, and his ideas had a genuine and altru-istic quality without offering an easy solution. You still had to

answer the very daunting individual question concerning what your life was about, and what you held most dear. It would be nice to find a way around that question, but why not take the time to think about what you really want?

The idea of "aligning yourself" sounds attractive, but it is not easily accomplished. It remains useless and it could drive you crazy trying to figure out why things are not working. In this day and age, authors, creative thinkers, and almost everyone who makes a big pile of money is doing so with a healthy dose of business sense and self-promotion. We all want a short cut, but inclusion of those qualities is essential, yet still, we are always looking for that short cut. It is the mythical journey of trying to turn lead into gold, or finding Aladdin's lamp, or winning the state lottery. But there are ways of improving your lot through a process that is not putting you at the mercy of the universe or God or unknown forces that are difficult to decipher, let alone harness.

Managing the Flow of It All

The state of having a great day is exhilarating, where one thing after another works out in your favor. A day when you get a contract for a book, and at the same time you sell a work of art, and also find that your father is getting out of the hospital, and that you just got a new freelance job, is one that you want to repeat. We have had many days like that, and in hindsight perhaps our optimistic attitude helped get us there. But also, we have had days when the opposite happened, that is, a loved one is having complications in the hospital, the bills aren't paid, and you are feeling sick. Why all these bad things at once?

The Book of Job & Suffering

In the book of Job, a great epic poem and story in the Old Testament, Job is a good man who fears God and goes to church every day. He has seven children and farms and is a wealthy man, by local standards, who gives generously to charities. As the story goes, God says to the Devil, "Have you seen my good servant Job?" The Devil replies that he has seen Job, and says that if Job were not in such a good material state of health and wealth he would despise God and not be such a "good servant." Then a strange bargain is made, proposed by God. God tells the Devil to do what he likes with Job, but not to kill him. Well, the Devil proceeds to do everything but kill him. God wagered that Job's faith would not waver amidst suffering.

Satan goes to it. First there are natural disasters and Job begins to lose his whole income from farming because of flash floods and fires. He continues to praise God. Then as his children are having a party in a house, the walls and roof collapse and they all die. They don't come back to life; they really die. He continues to praise God though He gives and takes away mysteriously. Finally, Job becomes sick and develops boils all over his body so that he is not comfortable in any position and must sit in ashes to be in the least amount of pain. That is the point when he breaks down and curses God. He wishes he were never born. He cries injustice, wondering how he can suffer when he is so truly good, while others who are wicked prosper. His friends try to comfort him telling him that he might want to look at it another way, because perhaps his suffering has a meaning he could not perceive. He eviscerates his friends' arguments by telling them that it is impossible for them to understand how much he suffers, and though Job says he would probably take their position if he was well, the fact that he is not well now makes a big difference in how he looks at life, or so he tells his friends.

God Appears

Job's argument is compelling and the reader identifies with Job and is looking forward to the end of the book when God appears. It is an epic poem that is very beautiful and one of the most troubling stories in the Bible. In the end God does appear. And with tremendous arrogance, God tells Job that he is essentially stupid (empty-headed), and that if Job knows so much, He challenges Job to explain how the sun sets and the moon rises. He challenges Job to answer questions beyond his comprehension and goes on to say that if he can't answer those questions, he has no right to spar with God over his suffering.

There are numerous ways to analyze this story, because Job does repent in the end, but his children are still dead, so what is the meaning of this tale?

Elie Wiesel, a great thinker and also a holocaust survivor, once said that it was odd that God never revealed to Job that it was all a game. Job was not at fault at all. He was the pawn in a bet between God and one of His fallen angels, Satan. Elie Wiesel was making a political analogy at the time to say that perhaps we are sometimes pawns in a larger political scheme and we mistakenly focus on the short-term needs of our lives, or even the marketing ploys of a government, rather than the greater truth.

Job Is a Story

Was Job not "in alignment" with the universe? No, Job is a story, not a motivational tale, a story to make the reader ponder the meaning of great gain and great loss—a story about fearing God; a story that questions modern notions of being in the great flow of life and achieving great things, and then falling out of that great flow or alignment. Perhaps the story is telling us that we must look outside our situation; we must look outside of ourselves (as Job was blind to the initial bet) and perhaps see larger forces at work. Or maybe the story is telling us we cannot see the forces that are really impacting our lives, that Job might be missing a key element in his analysis of the situation, like the fact that the meaning of our lives is not entirely about what we do, but how we think about it.

In the case of some of the great spins of our time, in the form of motivational self-help books, maybe it means to look at the means of production, at how such works and how the authors and the entrepreneurs achieved their success. That is the part of the game that we are not reading about, and instead we are seeing the results, which is confusing, just as the story of Job is confusing. It makes the reader contemplate a difficult question, which is the intention of this book as well.

The Criminal Mind and Morality

In Fyodor Dostoyevsky's *Crime and Punishment*, part of it was about a man who was justifying his crime of murder as different from others who committed murder, because he was an exceptional person, a thinker, a philosopher, not simply a common cold-blooded killer. He makes a compelling argument for a person who kills or commits a crime and has a sophisticated reasoning behind it, and suffers as well because he is sensitive enough to also understand the gravity of his action. It is a brilliant, thought-provoking book, and it has echoes in the current climate where people talk about getting "anything you want" through an understanding of how to harness the universal forces for your own personal needs. This begs the question: what if your purposes are criminal? Can you use the power of your mind to accomplish them? We know that masterful planning by criminal minds, as unethical as it is, can be carried off with incredible success.

We were living in New York during the devastating attacks on September 11th, on the World Trade Center. The amount of planning, with God supposedly on their side, was as incredible as all the things that had to align on that morning for those planes to have been flown almost at the same time and carried off as planned. Hitler was also able to commit extraordinary atrocities while the world's leaders turned their collective heads away for a long period of time, effectively allowing his plans to flourish.

Just as Rhonda Byrne may be a ruthless entrepreneur, the moral arc of getting what you want is weighed by all of us. What are we willing to do? How far will we go? What friendships are we willing to ruin? What small things are you willing to do to survive that may seem immoral to some?

Artistic License

As artists in New York City we had several friends who were not criminals but came close to this kind of behavior, and they shared their ideas for getting things for free.

The large chain store Bed, Bath & Beyond would take returns on absolutely anything, even if it was broken with missing parts. Once, we were able to buy all the materials we needed for an exhibit—lights, power cords, and more—only to return it all for a full refund when the show was over. For some artists, that was inappropriate at best, yet others were inspired by the idea. Is that something you would do? How far would you go in that direction?

One day we saw a broken fan laying on the street with the trash, and we knew it came from Bed, Bath & Beyond so we picked it up off the street and returned it for a full refund in store credit (about ninety bucks). Was it our lucky day? Yes, it was.

Some friends of ours were willing to do something else that other people's friends would not. Everybody has a limit. Other friends of ours were getting free coats and clothes from major retailers by doing something similar. They would walk into a chain store like The Gap, pull a coat off the rack that didn't have an electronic tab on it, and then would get in the returns line. They would present the coat they just pulled off the rack at the counter and say they wanted to exchange it for a different size and that they didn't have a receipt. They got what they wished for! A free coat, with a new bag and a new receipt saying it was an exchange so they could walk out the door. How unethical is that? How do we evaluate or justify these actions? Were Rhonda Byrne's actions so different from these tactics? We all draw the line in different places, but to define an act as "stealing" is not so simple. Consider how Apple Inc. avoids millions in taxes through loopholes, robbing the government and other taxpay-ers—why do we let that go, yet punish the petty thief?

Sneaking Around

The point here is that getting your wish has been a complex com-bination of things thus far, and may even include borderline illegal actions. In another example, film director Steven Spiel-berg likes to tell the story of how he got himself into the movie business. He would sneak onto the lot of a major film production studio by going in with a public tour. Then he would hide away there overnight.

In the morning he would go out for coffee and was sure to say hello to the security guard on his way out and back in. He was impersonating someone who worked there, illegally of course. In this manner, he was able to find a director and push his student script and get the attention he wanted which helped to launch his career. It was his big break that he himself obvi-ously created. Those were criminal actions, but in retrospect he sees them as heroic, and in this book we see them as part of what it takes to make your dreams come true, depending on how far you will go, or what you think is morally justified. That story that Spielberg told may even be a partial fabrication, but actors, as well as entrepreneurs, often force their way into situations to literally open doors that are closed.

The area of wishing for good things is written about enough, but wishing for bad things is the darker side of the equation. However, it takes the same type of guts and presence of mind that it takes to make good things happen. Even the morality of what it takes to get there is similar on both sides, because wanting good things to happen to you assumes that you feel deserving of those things.

CHAPTER 3

A Course in Miracles

THE BOOK THAT is the title of this chapter is one of the extraordinary spiritual texts of the twentieth century and it is little known outside of self-help circles and the New Age movement. It is a book that claims to teach how to perform miracles in detail. It also is a thorough and demanding course in mind training. As authors, we feel an affinity for this text that may border on displaying our own myopia on the subject. We have read it thoroughly and believe it is one of the very rare books that actually teaches the reader how to heal and how to perform miracles, and all without capitalist means. It is a truly spiritual book that trains the reader to reprogram his or her mind. It is not unlike other spiritual classics, which we will discuss.

Before we talk about what that means, and why it makes sense to us, consider how the book was written.

Hearing Voices

A Course in Miracles is an exception among books of new age spiritualism. The way it was written was itself a bit extraordinary. Helen Schucman wrote the book with the help of William Thetford, but they are not credited as authors because the book was dictated to Helen Shucman in the form of "voices," and in fact she claimed the voice she heard was that of Jesus.

As outrageous as that may sound, the background of the author, or better thought of as a "scribe" or messenger, sheds some light on the situation.

At the time, 1965, Thetford was director of the psychology department at Columbia-Presbyterian Medical Center in New York City. Schucman began her professional career at the Medical Center as Thetford's research associate, later also to become a tenured professor of psychology at Columbia University. They had become consultants on an interdisciplinary research project at the Cornell University Medical Center, Thetford's former employer. Their weekly meetings at the Center had become contentious, and they had described that they hated going, feeling both uncomfortable and angry. Tired of the competitiveness and negativity, on an afternoon in June 1965, Thetford delivered a speech to Schucman indicating that he felt they had been using the wrong approach. "There must be another way," he concluded. Schucman felt that this speech acted as a stimulus that triggered off a long series of inner experiences that could be categorized as visions, dreams, heightened imagery, and an "inner voice" that finally, on October 21, 1965, said to her: "This is a Course in Miracles, please take notes." She claims the voice identified itself as that of Jesus. Schucman said that the writing made her very uncomfortable, though it never seriously occurred to her to stop. Schucman explained what was happening to Thetford, who encouraged her to continue this process and helped her in typing out what she read to him from her notes the night before. The whole process took about seven years and gave us the book *A Course in Miracles.*

Authorless Book

That is a rather incredible story, and perhaps hard to believe, but it is how the book was written, and is not unlike how early Christians claimed to have written books that were dictated to them through messengers of God, sometimes depicted in Renaissance paintings as a dove whispering in the ear of the scribe. It is a leap of reason to understand this type of process. Esther Hicks also claims to be channeling or listening to the voice of Abraham in her writings, and there were the famous *Seth* series of books that also claimed to be written by a "voice" in the mind of the author or scribe.

It is difficult to authenticate this type of experience, similar to the problem of understanding any deeply personal experience such as how ideas come into a person's mind or how true inspiration works. J. K. Rowling says the idea for the entire series of *Harry Potter* books came to her quickly, almost in a flash. However, these are very different ideas than what is happening in *A Course in Miracles*, because in that book, the writing is so incredibly esoteric and unusual that something else seems to be truly at work.

Translations

When Thomas Jefferson was trying to create a good translation of the gospels in the Bible, he said it was a matter of reading through translations and finding what appeared to be authentic teachings. He compared the process to finding diamonds in a dung heap, that is, the original writing is so far superior to that of the translator's additions that it could be easily separated. In other words, a great teacher might pose riddles or give metaphors to teach but would probably not give out a list of do's and don'ts. So we can retranslate by seeking consistent quality.

Of course there could be many errors as well, but it is a worthwhile process because it supposes that a great teacher's writings could be damaged and mangled through bad translations, but the best concepts and ideas themselves would still remain in view and possible to separate from the rest by the sheer quality of the ideas.

After reading *A Course in Miracles*, and performing all the meditations it requires for 365 days, it does impart a profound sense of peace and also a theology that is unique; at least it did for us. Though Christian in many ways, it has rankled the majority of Christians who see it as near heresy for its view that you can directly talk with God, among other reasons. It seems to have more in common with Buddhism, but the book is too Christian in its views to be considered as such. It seems in effect to reach for the same pearl that so many religious thinkers are after—peace, not in the global sense, but inner peace that comes from knowing yourself and being consciously committed to self-discovery and self-realization. True peace of mind.

The introduction to the book contains this sentence, which helps to summarize the whole book: "Nothing real can be threatened. Nothing unreal exists. Herein lies the peace of God."

Before we discuss that sentence, which is a fascinating one, how can we trust a book that has been written in this way and what does that really mean? As readers of the book, we know that it has influenced many writers who have used the text to create a version based on it. Marianne Williamson was the most notable for her book *A Return to Love*, but many others mention the book and incorporate it into their teachings up to the current *May Cause Miracles*, by Gabrielle Bernstein.

A book that has been written by "channeling" or by hearing "voices," and has no author in the traditional sense, usually has a distinct sound to it. That sound, the tone of the book, is one written by an author without an ego or sense of self, as we know it. It is the way some great gurus write books that sound like a philosophical exercise, understanding that everything we see is a projection and an illusion. *A Course in Miracles* feels as if there is no author, or certainly one without the sense of self that we commonly read. You could say there are two kinds of books in the world, those written by authors and those that seem to have no author present in the writing. By "no author present" we do not mean that there is a narrator, but something quite distinct from that. It feels as if there is no ego, no sense of self, no self-conscious person authoring the book, but an all-knowing teacher. The New Testament of the Bible often has that ring to it but not always, due probably to bad translations of the great teachers. Let's look again at that introductory sentence and skip to the meaning of the whole book and how it teaches individuals to perform miracles.

"Nothing real can be threatened. Nothing unreal exists. Herein lies the peace of God."

This sentence begs the question "What is real?" The answer is given throughout the book, and knowing we will resist the answer, the book generates countless arguments to help fight that resistance and enable understanding. What is real, according to this book, is the fact that we are born innocent and remain innocent to our dying day. We may make mistakes, but we cannot change the essential nature of who we are. Then we are led through a series of arguments that persuade the reader to buy this concept: no matter what mistakes we make we are still as innocent as the day we were born.

What is "real" to us, the book argues, is not the physical world of the ego, and material reality; it is quite the opposite. The real things in this world are not the external world, and we are told that the external world is truly an illusion and the only one that is real is your interior world. If we can change how we perceive ourselves by consciously altering our perception, and adopting that concept, then indeed we can change the entire world around us. If we look at great stories of spiritual teachers like Jesus or Buddha, their examples will make this case clear. They did not operate under any of the guidelines that the authorities were imposing at that time. They chose to believe and preach that everything is within us. The kingdom is within us, the world is all illusion, so follow God, or yourself, and you will see the truth for yourself and will know it when it is found.

Unlike most books of this genre, which end up perverting the message by turning it into something often self-serving, *A Course in Miracles*, we feel, is the real deal, authentic, the essence of what many self-help books ideally try to teach. In many other books, though parts of any pure message can come through, it often ends up confusing, just like a bad translation of a great teacher's writing, and we are left hanging, trying to understand what the writing means, like the phrase "alignment with the universe," for example.

How Miracles Are Performed

According to *A Course in Miracles*—a text that echoes religious thinking throughout the ages with a seemingly pure intention—

it is within our power to perform miracles and there is a method to making miracles happen. However, the book states that a miracle could be performed and it is possible nothing will happen that is obvious. The way that book tells the reader to perform a miracle is by using a simple phrase. If you are sick or are feeling dragged down by various fears or other conditions, you must close your eyes, meditate for a moment and say to yourself, while really believing the sentiment, *I have no need for this*. If you are performing a miracle on someone else who is sick or dying, the same thing happens only if you say it to yourself silently while in the presence of the other person, with hands on them or not, "You have no need for this." The book goes on to say that this phrase and action might cause spontaneous healing and it might seem to do nothing at all, but the miracle is performed nevertheless. For the purpose of this book, this is one of the profound experiences that you could in fact use or call upon.

Innocence

The reason that those few words, "I have no need for this," carries such potential weight is that they are based on the hundreds of pages in the book that make an argument for your essential innocence. This is a very important point that we think wishes are based on, as well as miracles, and probably much of what makes so many new age proclamations either function or fail. It may also shed light on the idea of what it means to "align yourself" with the universe.

The ideas that are argued in *A Course in Miracles*, with profound intelligence, are that we cannot be separated from God or the Oneness or the larger Self that we are. One way or another, we must perceive our innocence, and thereby gain true peace of mind and experience no guilt of any kind. Realizing our innocence is setting the stage for understanding what forgiveness really means, and how to believe it when you are forgiving someone. It is a more complex issue than it first appears to be, because to forgive someone entirely is the same as forgiving yourself entirely, and that is really where the miracle happens. Because to do that means that you think that true forgiveness is possible, that is, you have to know that it is possible to perceive yourself as completely innocent. Most of us feel that is not the case, and that somehow, somewhere in us, there is a darkness, or that we have done something wrong in the past, or have intentions that are not always, shall we say, enlightened.

Pure Heart

To become enlightened and to have a pure heart, that is, one without regret, you must train yourself in a way to get to that point. For us, *A Course in Miracles* is one way, but there are also many other ways. The unusual thing about enlightenment or a pure mind that can easily forgive in the fullest sense of the word, is that it is possible for it to happen in an instant. Yes, a mind-training course may work, but it can also be learned in a windfall of information, a moment of "seeing" the truth. This is historically how it is said to have come to many people and great teachers. In part, this is where the confusion lies. Can we gain all of this instantly or does it take time? That is a question that is both yes and no, and like any spiritual quest, it is in the seeking that you find a multitude of answers. The course in this book and the dialogue on the schoolofwishing.com website offers a community of feedback to help you with your own process and path.

Meditations

As with many Eastern religious concepts, there is an acknowledgment that all our worries and fears are self-induced, and that we project all of these fears onto the world around us. If we are afraid, then the world is a fearful place, and if we are happy and secure, the world is a place of support and safety.

A Course in Miracles may be a bit rigorous for many people to adhere to, because it asks for you to perform daily meditations, but a process like that can alter the way we perceive our surroundings. And it is that very state of mind in which we feel wishes and desires can be created, nurtured, and brought to fruition.

It is also a state where you suspend your current beliefs for the moment.

Just as we were saying in the first chapter about the means to prove a miracle the way the Vatican does, you can almost think about your own miracles in the same way. There are tangible miracles such as health and healing that can be quantified and proven to a large degree, but then there are miracles that are internal which are harder to examine. Such a miracle might be the understanding of something you previously did not understand, like a sudden bolt of realization, an "aha" moment, or as simple as suddenly forgiving someone for something. How do we measure what we know is entirely personal? Given this reasoning, we know we have miracles running through us all the time. How does a poem or joke make an impact? How do we find the strength to forgive or turn the other cheek?

Investigation

There are so many things happening inside us that are hard to understand, and impossible to prove, but we know they are happening. There is a level of proof we all need to believe in something. Yes, we want to see facts and an investigation into supposed real-life miracles, but when they happen to us, we don't think that same kind of proof is necessary. To make other people believe it we might want proof, but for ourselves we don't. In this context there are miracles happening to all of us every day, if we become aware of it.

Today, we have witnessed a few miracles already, in this sense. This morning was beautiful for no reason at all. It was a day like any other day, but as breakfast was being made there was a feeling that this will be a great day because we were feeling a lot of energy and enthusiasm. Where did that come from, is that a miracle? Yes, it is a miracle perhaps, a powerful change or adjustment in our mood and outlook and that made all the difference in our functioning! It has no known source. Was it dinner last night or was it because there was no dinner last night? Was it because we received a check? (We hadn't received a check or financial windfall.) Was it because we had a good night's sleep?

We can only guess at it, but like inspiration itself, there is no recipe to make it occur on command, though we have many maps to point us in the direction we need to go, and this book is one of them.

Every day miracles are formed and created by our ability to notice and focus our attention on what is happening now. Miracles could be a change in mood, or a gift, or a recovery from illness, or even the smallest detail, like your shoes fitting well. There are minor and major miracles for sure, but we can look at a variety of levels and see that it is happening all around us, all the time.

CHAPTER 4

Changing Your Beliefs

TO TRANSFORM YOURSELF into something differ-
ent, perhaps more peaceful, more ambitious, or just a completely
new outlook on life can either take a lot of time or very little at all.

A good example of instant change, as opposed to changing your spiritual and material life slowly, is the way many people overcome addictive behaviors. A friend who was an active
alcoholic and drug abuser talks about how everyone has a different "all-time-low point." He was responding to a question
about how to help someone with a drug addiction. He said that
you cannot help someone until they want to be helped. This is
a crucial statement that you may have heard before, but it is a
different process for everyone. For that friend, even though he
had been an alcoholic and drug abuser for decades, the event
that turned him around was being stopped by the police while

driving drunk, only to be let go with guns and marijuana in the car. After that wake-up call, he decided to quit everything and terminate all his old habits to lead a brand new life and way of being with the help of the organization Alcoholics Anonymous. He has been sober for five years now. Another person we know talks about a friend who was using crack cocaine for over a decade; how one day the addict said to a friend that he hated his life as it was, and the next day he quit using drugs and has been clean and sober for the past three years.

You may or may not have an addictive nature, but you probably have learned habits that are well ingrained in your personality. They can be changed instantly, or over time.

Low Point

Changing those habits to become a different or better person can be easy or it can be hard. What is your turning point? What is your "all-time-low point"? What is the equivalent of your all-time-low? What event or realization will it take to make you commit to a change? We know it can occur at any age, and if an addict can quit and change their life completely at sixty years old, you can change any habit if you really want to. It is not just a possibility, it happens every day.

Maybe thinking about the meaning of life, as Victor Frankl observes it, will help. Thinking of the question of why you are living this life will help to shape your thoughts. If it is for a career goal like getting your art in a museum, publishing a book, or taking care of your kids, that is a good place to begin.

Family Life

Let's say you decide your life is about seeing your kids grow up and making sure they have what they need in terms of your support to do so. If that is your firm decision, then what must be done next? You are already raising them of course, but what do you need to do to make sure they have an exceptional experience with you as a parent?

That could be a turning point, depending on how seriously you want and wish to craft something for your child or another person in your life. Perhaps you want to be a role model of fairness, or an example of ambition and education. Whatever it is, if this is truly what your life is about, why not dedicate yourself to perfecting the meaning therein? In the case we are discussing about a child, it could mean a variety of things. Perhaps you want to see your child happy and fulfilled, and then the next step is the details, the actions of creating that situation. What activities do you want to see or share? What do you want the child to experience? We are turning your wishes for the future into a reality by directing your thoughts and actions toward goals that will satisfy you and possibly change the lives of everyone around you.

If you have a professional goal, like getting a better job or a similarly ambitious idea about your art or music being sold, there are actions that would go along with that as well. The idea of taking a new, determined direction can happen in an instant or it could take longer. The missing part of most texts on changing yourself is to decide what are the next actions to take, which are often bold, extroverted, and entrepreneurial.

Big Questions

The question remains, what will it take for you to change the course of your life to make vast improvements and watch your wishes take form?

There are several ways to begin to reprogram who you are, to be a better, more efficient person in matters of love, work, and internal joy. All these are areas where wishes are made. It begins with a method to track your current thoughts and change them as well as beginning a new regimen of mental exercises. Neuro-Linguistic Programming (NLP) took a great leap forward with books like Bandler and Grinder's *The Structure of Magic Volumes I and II*. It was the start of what is known as the Human Potential Movement and it influenced many people, including Tony Robbins, who used the material of NLP for his own motivational lectures and teachings.

Some ideas, some books, some moments in life just seem to come at the right time. There are many stories of people being inspired by a book or an event, and perhaps this is your moment, or maybe not, but if you are reading this book you are in search of that, and sooner or later it will come, that is, you will find words or an experience that changes your life forever. This book is called the *School of Wishing*, so if you picked it up, it is because you want to learn, you liked the title perhaps, and that is a powerful and potent start that points in a direction.

Tennis

Let's look at the story of Serena and Venus Williams, and how an event did not change their lives, but how a way of thinking, a type of mind training that was very effective, quite possibly did.

Making dreams come true is in the story of the extraordinary rise of African American tennis stars Venus and Serena Williams. There have been books and movies about their lives, but from a recent interview with their father and coach, Richard Williams, we learned something unusual, many things really, but one thing in particular.

When their father was promoting them, he would make posters announcing their local games as if they were famous already, while in fact they were not famous at all yet, they were young children. He would also tell them a typical line from an

inspirational speaker whom he admired. He would say, "you are famous today and will be a celebrity by Friday." Talk about motivational! The father is assuming they are already famous, and have just a few more steps to go to be international celebries. One of the sisters commented on this process and said that "the combination of belief and training were unconquerable." Let's look at this for a moment, because while there were other factors involved in their success, like supportive parents who were heavily invested in the game, the sisters also acted as though they had already arrived. This is a concept that multiple New Age gurus like Wayne Dwyer talk about. In general, they say to act and think as if you are already in possession of what it is that you want.

Fake It to Make It

In the case of the Williams sisters, they acted as if they were already famous, but an important ingredient that is left out of the many teachings of this attitude is the hard training they did every day. The sisters woke up at 6 A.M. and practiced before going to school, and then after school they continued to practice. The unconquerable combination was the fact that they believed they had already arrived, not that they were sure they would make it, but that it was already a done deal. The hard work in the form of training is the element that makes a winning combination with an attitude that was formed by their father's illusions, or delusions, that certainly became a reality.

We would all like a genie to actually give us three wishes that require nothing more than asking, but even if we believe all that we read in the latest books on wishing your way to success, there is hard work involved as well. Oftentimes, extraordinarily hard work, with the constant and nearly pathological belief that you will make it or that, in fact, you have *already* made it, helps the mind to persevere and adopt a stance that can resist the various bumps along the road to any wish being fulfilled.

Mind-Training Alternatives

There are numerous books that may help you in your quest, but there is a danger in over thinking and you have to work very hard to avoid this as well. The process of getting what you want can also come much easier. One method is to think about what it is that you do want. Like Victor Frankl said, think about the reason you are living. What is it that you really want? That may come to you very easily, but it might not. If it is not coming to you, and you think that you need to do more soul-searching, then reading more will help, and the course material near the end of this book should also help. Another alternative is to play a bit more, have fun in some way, and see if it comes to you instantly.

Playful Attitude and Actions

There are always mind-training exercises, and we will get to some soon, but the other method is to play. While we are laughing, or doing something truly fun that allows us to forget everything and leave it all behind, we are in an elevated state that is close to what you are searching for. "Some have entered the kingdom laughing" has a beautiful sound to it in this context, because laughter allows us to release our self-conscious thoughts and permits something more divine to enter; our dreams, our lightest thoughts can emerge in laughter. The trick to playing your way to finding out what it is that you want is to reflect after play. After you ride on a rollercoaster, for example, and are laughing with friends about how scared you were, when you are home, re-create that moment by remembering it and running it through your head again with your eyes closed. When you do this you will find that some of the experience comes back to you in a physical form, that is, besides smiling at the memory, you will actually re-create a part of the experience physically for yourself, yet you are alone in a chair. When you do this, let your mind wander, and see where it goes, knowing you are looking for a pointer to hint at what it is you truly want.

Selfless Gestures

We are living in a culture that makes so much out of our personal needs and wants. Perhaps to fulfill ourselves we can also consider not just private gains, but the gains of those all around us. When Victor Frankl spoke about his desire to write a book, it was an altruistic idea, a desire to help others. Even the desire to see your children grow up is one outside the realm of yourself.

So when you are sitting there trying to re-create an experience of joy, and looking for pointers to a fulfilling life, it may mean that you might help an organization, or maybe that you will volunteer, or start your own community group for supporting others. One rather odd but wonderful example is the client of a therapist we know. The therapist was telling us how there are so many ways to do what you love, and one man that she was working with told her that all he really liked to do was to talk about sports all the time! He said if he could find a way to talk about baseball and football all day he would be in heaven. What he ended up doing was to turn a passenger van into a transportation service to baseball and football games. He would drive, and also go to the games, and spent the majority of his time talking about sports to his passengers, going to every game, and getting a full-time salary from it! It's a wonderful example because it would seem that you can't make a living just talking about something, but his goal was met by doing something related. He could have been a sports announcer, or a vendor at sports games, but that wasn't a good fit for him and wouldn't involve enough financial and intrinsic reward. He decided on a simple plan that put him in charge and gave him everything he wanted. Don't you think there is a solution like that for all of us? We just have to find it.

CHAPTER 5

Why Wishing Is Better Than Trying

THERE ARE A lot of things in this life we try to do, but fail. It is inherent in the word "try." We can try to get a job, or try to achieve our dream, and the irony is that we will succeed at trying, and at the same time fail to reach our goal, because "to try" only means to attempt something. You could say that you will try to write a book. Then you can spend time each day trying without a word written down. After a while you can conclude that you did in fact "try" and actually, you succeeded at trying, and at the same time failed to write your book. This does not mean that you shouldn't try something new, but you must be aware that failure is almost written within that word, because you can succeed at trying and never come close to your goal.

Wishing, on the contrary, will get you closer to what you really want, because there is a subtle but important difference.

Like trying, you can also wish successfully without getting anything, but you hold open the possibility of the wish being fulfilled at any time in the future. There is a difference here that is important, because with trying it is either hopeful or hopeless. If we succeed at trying, but fail at achieving our goal, it is hopeless to try again, or at least not very hopeful. But if we are wishing for something and it doesn't come true, we know that it may come true in the future; it is a hopeful situation even though there are no grounds to be hopeful. The doors have not closed and a wish can always come true, so it is better than trying, which is often a dead end.

To be hopeful is the prime objective of a wish, and to "try" something is really more of an experiment. So if hope is the game you want to play then you have to learn to let more of it into your life. Being hopeful, or optimistic, is something that we are all born with. It is a sense of innocence about the world and the possibilities that are there for all of us. As a child, almost everyone feels that there are endless possibilities for the future.

Optimism vs. Blame

As we get older, it becomes easy to be bitter and less optimistic when we have been through so many difficult trials of life. Some remain optimistic, but most feel the pressure of a global economy that is suffering, and we are playing much less, and how easy it is to complain about the success of others and blame the world for our woes. Even the most intelligent people blame their parents and everything else around them, and in fact, being smart and knowing it can be one of the most embittering experiences when there is little money to show for it. This is normal. We age, we learn, and often the lessons are not kind and we struggle with relationships, stress, and our inability to achieve what we thought we were going to achieve at a younger age. Time seems to cease to be a friend and the pressure increases.

Time

Having a child was one notion that changed our minds about the amount of time we had left to change ourselves. We were adults in our twenties, having a child, and did not feel we could change careers as freelance artists, but simply had to make more money to support our child. But something changed when we thought about his future. From the moment we began caring for him, he would grow, and within seventeen or eighteen years he will have a whole new set of skills, a fresh outlook on life, and everything ahead of him. As we pondered those numbers, we were struck by something. Since he would really not be pursuing his interests until at least twelve years old, the years from twelve until he reaches the age of matu-

rity is about seven years. That is, in seven years of high school and college, he will learn so much that he can design an entire life from it, and enter into a new field with hope. Don't we all have seven years? I think we do, no matter how old you are, and it will probably take much less. You are already an adult, and if you are interested in a complete change, it is possible. A college degree takes four years, and that is a life-changing experience. We began to think differently watching our child grow. We realized just as we will watch him pursue and learn the skills of a new career, we could do the same. Since we are primarily visual artists, we decided we would like to be writers as well. We knew nothing about the industry and had the same feelings and dreams like other artists, of wanting to share our knowledge with passion, but in our case we realized we actually had time to do it. It was not so much the time during the day, but the realization that we had at least seven years to pursue a whole new life and learn what is necessary for that life. That was a feeling of new-found optimism, a sense of hope, the opposite of the pressing feeling we had to raise our child and find the money needed to give him a life of possibilities. We had something to look forward to.

We were not about to go to college again, so the cheaper alternative was to read everything we could about the publishing industry. In less than five years from that point we had an agent and a publisher and this is now our fourth book. It is what we wished for, but what gave us hope in the possibility of its coming true was knowing we had time to make it happen, the belief that time was indeed on our side. We also spent that time learning and reading and doing.

Belief

Many of us wishers and dreamers want to believe so badly in magical things, in wonders yet undiscovered, that we can easily be hoodwinked. There was a video called "Liquid Mountaineering (Walk on Water)" that now has over twelve million views on YouTube and is a good example of how we suspend disbelief so that we can think the impossible can happen. The video was very well produced and is in fact a gimmick for a shoe company. In the video, there are a few guys who run fast and think they can run on water. It is produced in such a way that looks like it could be low budget and these guys are just making a great YouTube video. We watch the runners sprint straight for the shoreline and attempt to run on water in a small lake only to fail and fall in. Then we see snippets of interviews and how they are saying you have to believe it is possible, and we see a slow-motion version of what looks like two or three steps on water while running before they fall in. It is compelling and it looks like a miracle of faith is happening. There is not an obvious shoe sponsor, but the logo is everywhere, on the hats of the people talking and of course the shoes when we see them. Finally at the end of the video, which is about three minutes in length, we see runners taking several steps on water. The truth is that there was a transparent bridge just under the surface of the water that was creating the illusion. It was false, a lie, an illusion that took advantage of our willingness and desire to believe in the miraculous.

Illusion

It is a brilliant video, and when we first saw it, we believed it, and thought that the power of believing you can do something is in itself extraordinary. We watched the video over and over, and it told us exactly what we wanted to hear and never let on to the fact that it was completely false.

Our son was amazed, and we shared it on Facebook. On YouTube there were compilations of videos where people did incredible things, like long jumps, tricks with bicycles and skateboards, and more, and a clip from running on water was also included. It had quickly become part of our cultural language of everyday heroics by average people.

The disappointment was poignant when we found it to be a hoax. Though it was a wonderful video, when it was revealed that it was a fraudulent commercial by a shoe company, there was a lot of anger in the comments. We felt the same way. It is the high-tech equivalent of a snake oil salesman. In this day and age, it works even better if a product isn't mentioned. It became a viral sensation and took advantage of our ability to suspend our skeptical nature to believe in the miraculous. It is also a sign that we have to dig deeper when looking at what appears to be a solution or example of dreams coming true.

Critical Thinking

A critical examination of any new method to make miracles happen is necessary, and though it seems to be a bit sad, and even incites anger when you are fooled, it is to be expected. Now that we are living in an age where viral videos are being produced daily, our willingness to believe is being tested. At the same time, we are faced with the difficult task of being open and optimistic in these circumstances.

Our past experiences are largely what we use to analyze the truth of a situation. So when we look at videos we are more skeptical, and the Internet allows us to get a variety of opinions rather quickly. Just type in the title of any video or even the subject line of a bulk email you got from a relative and you will have a good chance at finding the truth of its origin, and that makes all the difference. It can be very subtle, but knowing when you are intentionally being deceived is helpful. Now when we get a joke email, as we did last week from a relative to about sixty people, which claims that the late astronaut Neil Armstrong said some cryptic things during the moon landing, we search for the truth of it. We type in the subject of the email with the words "true or false" next to it, and usually discover which it is. In the case of the Neil Armstrong joke, it was not true, though it sounded plausible and was funny.

CHAPTER 6

Wishing and Praying

THE TOP MOST-WISHED-FOR things come in a great variety of forms. As we researched wishes on the Internet, we found a variety of sites that allow people to post wishes and prayers anonymously. There is a wonderful and slightly sad feeling when reading through so many wishes, because we often wish for something when the situation is dire, and although that is not always the case, it is part of what gives a wish a sense of urgency and need. There are wishes floating all over the Internet, and in some ways they are very similar to prayers.

When we first met each other (the authors of this book) we began living together in a small storefront in the East Village of Manhattan. We are not religious believers in the strict sense, but prayer has always struck us as a powerful act even if it doesn't get the results you are after. In our storefront, we opened the doors once a week and gave away hugs, as well as bandages for non-visible wounds and also foot-washings for anyone who would come in. You could say it was our spiritual form of religion, or community service, but really it was simply something we wanted to do, something we wanted to practice. We are also artists, so that was what gave us the sense that we could just open our doors and do that, artistic license, so to speak.

Artistic Notoriety

It turned out that we became very well known for these acts and were eventually invited to major museums to do the same actions of giving away hugs and washing people's feet. However, we did something else at that time, which had a profound effect on us, and it was called *Pray For Me*. We put a sign on our storefront door that said PRAY FOR ME, and there were little pieces of paper that people could fill out and write their prayers on. They could write anything at all, and in hindsight, it was actually what they were wishing for to a great extent.

After they filled out the small piece of paper with their prayer on it, they would put the paper through our mail slot in the door and we would read the prayers and pray for them as best we could. There was also a spot on the paper form to fill in your email address, so if people did leave their email, we would send them a note after we had prayed for them telling them we had done so. We thought it would be nice to get an email saying that your prayer had been performed. As it turned out, people loved that.

Prayers Answered

As we began reading all of these prayers, it made us smile, laugh, and at times it was very poignant and nearly brought us to tears. Because the process was anonymous with the exception that they would leave their email address sometimes, people would often say exactly what was going on that hurt them most or was painful. There were prayers asking for a range of things from the ability for a relative to overcome alcoholism, or a sick child to be healed, to the more mundane, like a new dog, or more money, or a promotion at work. These prayer requests were a window into what other people needed most desperately. The phrase "Pray for Me" suggests a bit of desperation and a desire to be changed, to be healed—or to be heard, at the very least.

Prayers, Wishes, and the Will to Change

Praying and wishing are very closely related, but are distinctly different from the idea of "willing" something to happen. When we pray we are asking someone, or a deity of some kind, to intervene on our behalf and help us. If we are praying for rain, or for a better job, we are assuming that there is a way we can open a dialogue with a greater power so that we can gain the favor of, or help from, something outside ourselves. The idea of a conversation, a plea like this, is attractive in itself because we are expressing and giving voice to something we want, we need, and is at the top of our list. Historically this is a conversation with God, but prayer can be a conversation with any type of spiritual entity that you think could help you. If you are praying for inner strength, or for the will to go on with something, you are asking for help to muster your own power, but that conversation might also be with your own self, which has a distinct persona that you may be at odds with.

If you are struggling with a moral decision, there can be an inner critic that is advising you one way, while you rationalize the other way. Who do you listen to? The dialogue a prayer sets up could be with these types of inner beings that we can easily imagine. If we are asking for more internal strength or even more physical strength, then we are looking for a source to tap into that strength and to cast our loyalty to one side, that is, the inner being urging you on and confirming your desire.

Magical Properties of Wishing

Wishing is similar to praying but has some clear differences. When we wish on a star, or over the candles on a birthday cake, we are not battling inner demons or petitioning a higher force like God or even our greater self to intervene. We are assuming that a wish is like magic, that it is like telling a genie who just granted you three wishes your first wish. The content of your wish may be the same as the content with a prayer, but the intermediary is very different. In fact, when wishing, unless there is a genie in front of you, there is no intermediary, it is only you and the universe, and you hope it will make things right somehow, you hope your wish will come true.

When praying, of course, someone is ideally listening to your prayer, and you are heard. Beyond that, it is supposed that upon hearing that prayer, it will be answered. The third element here is the role of your will.

Will It to Happen

Your will, or ability to use your will, is one of the things that being in "alignment" might point to. When we talked about the authors of other books and how they became a success in their own right, it was not merely from wishing or using a secret formula; they were also driven entrepreneurs who were using their will and business expertise to achieve what they wanted. Using your will is the ability to keep a goal in mind, like making a business idea successful by taking specific action steps to put a plan into action. It is what drug and alcohol addicts use to

stop. Your ability to use your will might become clear by understanding what it means to "have no will." If you have no will it means that you are blown around by circumstances that are as unpredictable as the weather. You may know what it is that you would like to do, such as find a better job or write a book, but you haven't the will to do it because circumstances are beyond your control. You are in a default mode where things keep "happening" to you. Whether external things are truly beyond your control is something the individual must answer, but it often appears as though we have less control than we actually do. This is where your will is an important element.

As Seth Godin, the author and business blogger, said in a recent post, "If you can't influence the outcome, ignore the possibility. It's merely a distraction."

The full quote is below, but he is pointing to the role of will and effort alone to achieve your means because wishing for your dream or ideal future could be or is, in fact, a useless distraction according to him.

This is from the blog of Seth Godin and is a sobering thought from a well-regarded author on business practices, strategies, and markets.

It may be true that wishes are a waste of time, but what about when they work or seem to work? People have wished on the lottery and won clearly. But, by far, more people have lost. Nevertheless some did wish and got their wish. So let's look at that. Though it's a minority, we know people get their wishes sometimes despite the slim odds, right? Therefore, it is working for them and has changed lives in many cases.

As Godin states in "The Wishing/Doing Gap":

> It would be great to be picked, to win the random lottery, to have a dream come true.
>
> But when we rely on a wish to get where we want to go, we often sacrifice the effort that might make it more likely that we get what we actually need. Waiting for the prince to show up is a waste of valuable time, and the waiting distracts us from and devalues the hard work we might be doing instead.
>
> If you can influence the outcome, do the work.
>
> If you can't influence the outcome, ignore the possibility. It's merely a distraction.

Godin is not closing the door on wishing, but is saying to be sure you are doing the appropriate, real physical work that you need to do. As many other writers of self-help books have said, "you need to be in alignment," but that is really referring to *where* your wishes are headed. You need a good business structure and plan as well.

In other words, you will need to keep wishing while also doing some serious planning.

The combination of these two opposing systems of thought causes one issue of confusion on the matter. That is, how can we hope for something, knowing it might be hopeless? It might be the role of denial, but as human beings we want to believe in something against the odds, we want to prove the scientists wrong, and take a new route, even in the face of impossibility. Consider the state lottery for example. The odds are incredibly slim that you will win big, but we know that some people do win very big and that they were not doing anything special other than buying tickets every day! What is the name for something like that? Is it luck?

The Luck of the Irish

Luck is a phenomenon that is known to be random, though appears as though it is consistent, or that you are "on a roll," so to speak. We may in fact have periods of luck as well as its opposite, but how do they determine our fate? In a recent interview, the young Hollywood star and lead actor in *The Amazing Spiderman* movie in 2012 was asked how his career became so big in such a short time. With a disarmingly smart reply, the British actor was thoughtful and said that he felt he could really only attribute his success to luck. Not that he didn't work hard he said, "but that things like the color of your hair matter."

This is a tough lesson for an aspiring actor—hard work is good, but luck is nearly everything, including timing and circumstances beyond your control, like the way you look.

How long can we remain open to luck before we begin feeling like we have had an unlucky life? Can we remain perpetually open to luck somehow?

History shows us through stories, as well as the news, that those who least expect it often get a windfall of help and resources. We know there is no recipe to generate that consistently, but because of those stories, we remain hopeful. A battle cry might be: We can wish, can't we?

The Non-Visible Adventure— The Museum of Non-Visible Art

As authors, and as artists, we often wish for things that seem improbable, to test the limits of our own creativity and powers. As we mentioned earlier, we are artists who work together as a collaborative called Praxis. We received wide recognition in art museums for giving out hugs and foot-washings. As of 2013, and beyond, we are working on something we call the Museum of Non-Visible Art. The first part of this book will end with this story, because before you start the course you should know that when we talk about thinking outside the sphere of perception as

we know it, we mean *way outside* the sphere. This is an example
of how we convert our creative thinking into practice. It may be
useful to know so that you can lift any and all limits on what is
possible for you to wish up.

We decided to start a project, an art project called MONA, or
the Museum of Non-Visible Art. It was in the summer of 2011 that
it began with a Kickstarter project to raise money and awareness
for what we were doing. The idea was that we would create a world
where people could make artworks that cannot be seen with your
eyes but can be described and enjoyed the way traditional art is.
Instead of using your eyes, you use your mind's eye.

If you owned a work of non-visible art, you would show it to
someone in the following manner. You would have a card on the
wall that describes the art (any type of artwork or any medium).
Printed out nicely on a foam-core type card, it would be affixed
to the wall next to an empty space and would briefly describe the
artwork in seventy-five words or less, with a title, a date, and
the name of the artist who made it. For example, you would walk
over to the card and tell the viewer that the card says this is a
painting by Jeff X titled "Landscape in Maine," and it is oil on
canvas, 4 x 5 feet, and it is a landscape of a sunset in a field with
a horse and rider. The card goes on to describe the work and may
say something like this: "On a cloudy day a horse and a rider are
galloping through a field with a setting sun in the distance, and
when the sun sets they become a public sculpture made out of
white ceramic. The rider has a smile on her face while the horse
is mid-stride." It may have a few more words of description, but

not much more than that. As you tell the viewer what the painting is, the viewer then looks at the blank wall and imagines the field and the sunset and the horse and rider.

As the owner of the work you can add some of the detail that you might see, such as birds flying overhead or a dog running by. Perhaps the viewer says she or he sees tall trees as well, or another rider in the background. It is all part of the experience of looking at and imagining non-visible art in your home. Now the viewer understands how non-visible art works, and they could conceivably buy a work as well. They would take it to their house, put the description on the wall, and describe it to their friends.

Non-Visible Sales and Success

If you are following along this far, you might be thinking that this is an interesting exercise of some sort, but can we sell this non-visible art? The function of sales in this instance is very important to us, because when something is sold and exchanged, namely art, it gives it real value in the marketplace. Our next step with MONA was to have a Kickstarter project and see if we could sell the non-visible work by giving buyers the card we just described and a letter of authentication. We priced the artworks from $25 to $10,000. It turned out, with a little promotional push through social media, and the collaboration of a well-known person, it became a big success, selling over $16,000 worth of non-visible art and getting lots of press as well.

It went so well that now we are working on hiring an architect to design more museums around the world to house non-visible art. You can see this all online, and for us it is truly one of our biggest dreams that we have great passion for. It is all happening and coming true in very real terms because we are not only serious wishers, but are also creative people determined to change the way the world perceives art and the way people perceive their own power to create.

In the next chapter we begin the course on wishing, if you are ready, from our School of Wishing.

We wish you success!

Part ②

CHAPTER 7

The School of Wishing

The Wishing Exchange

Social media platforms like Twitter and Vine allow users to make wishes and send them out into the world like a note in a bottle in the sea. They may come back in the form of blessings and wishes granted; they may not come back at all. But to hashtag a wish (#schoolofwishing) can't hurt and might even help that wish to come true. To hashtag a wish is to be in the social media world of wishing. It is a positive place and also an altruistic one, a place of empathy and compassion.

You are entering the School of Wishing (link those words to www.schoolofwishing.com) and your eleven-day course begins here. The link above takes you to the page where you can see more resources that we keep updating, including additional course material.

This is now your handbook, a course that will send you wishing into a world that seems to be encouraging everything but wishing. Be prepared by being brave as well as thoughtful.

Become a Teacher

This is an eleven-day course, it might take a year or just eleven days—that's up to you—but it is a master's course, meant to transform your potential and behavior, to orient you to a greater goal, a greater good, which is like wishes coming true. When you complete this chapter and participate in the online blog about the course, or share your wish in any number of ways, we will send you a diploma from the School of Wishing, beautifully printed and ready for framing. This piece of paper will certify you as a graduate and allow you to teach wishing everywhere your heart desires. It is a form of encouragement because we believe that a world full of more wishers would be a better, more peaceful place.

This eleven-day course is to be completed in as much time as it takes you. There is a brief version of each day, in case you do not want to do all the reading, but it is like almost any learning experience. You will notice results right away, though if you make it a lifestyle, miracles can truly happen and your learning could become a catalyst for something greater than you have imagined.

The objective of this course is to make you an expert, to the degree that you are able, at wishing and also to enable you to teach others the same process of wishing with true passion. There are enough wishes for all of us, and the more this course circulates, the more wishes will come true, because more wishes will be made which naturally means, by the sheer number of them, that more will come true. It is an endless exchange, a type of perpetual motion machine of wishes being generated for other people and for you.

A World of Wishing Teachers

Can a world full of wishing teachers really do any harm? If wishing were taught in universities and elementary schools, with the goal of getting us all to think so far out of the box that we were wishing for things that could never exist, would that be helpful? We think so. There is enough sorrow and sadness in this world, and besides attempting to achieve our own dreams, we all need to practice helping others to achieve theirs. We can wish great things for others. Early prophets, from Jesus to Buddha, talked about giving in order to receive. Today, we have a whole school of thinkers from Deepak Chopra and Rhonda Byrne to Adam Grant in his book, *Give and Take*. It has always been emphasized in self-help books and other texts that as we help others, we also help ourselves. The more we give to others and make them happy, the more happiness is returned to us and therefore makes us happier. It becomes a circle, a wonderful circle of happiness.

Thus, if you choose to take the course and be a teacher of wishing, you can expect wonderful things in return.

Using the Course

This course has required reading, which you are meant to enjoy, question, and understand. For fruitful class discussions, or questions, see our blog at www.schoolofwishing.com. In order to complete this course and receive a diploma, these books must be read.

The books have selections and specific chapters assigned, but feel free to read all the chapters if you can, because it is being used to build your knowledge base of how other cultures use wishes, which are very close to prayers and meditation. These books will collectively teach the student the cultural history, as seen through major theological texts, of the way in which wishing has been used, and how to understand its consistent properties and teach others the same.

This course is meant to change your life. Really? Really. Why else do it? When wishes come true sometimes things don't change radically. They should, and if they don't, that becomes radical too in a way, because wishes are running against the grain of what you can expect, and it is against the grain of what is possible or practical. It is a dreamer's art. This is the course to master becoming that type of dreamer. It is greater than belief; it is closer to magic.

List of books to read for discussion, in this order:

The Ingenious Gentleman Don Quixote of La Mancha, by Miguel de Cervantes—Introduction and chapters one through five

The Interpretation of Dreams, by Sigmund Freud—Introduction and chapter three

I Am That, by Nisargadatta Maharaj—Introduction and chapter one

A Course in Miracles—Preface, Introduction, chapter one, pages 3–6 only; the section titled "Workbook for students," pages 1–3 only; continue to do the exercises daily, one day for each exercise on pages 4, 5, 6, and pages 8, 10, and 11

Autobiography of a Yogi—Introduction and chapter one

Tao Te Ching—the first six poems

The Bible (Jerusalem Bible or other edition)—Book of Job and the Old Testament

Give and Take: A Revolutionary Approach to Success, by Adam M. Grant, PhD—chapters one through three

Supplies needed for the student:

1. This book.
2. Optional smartphone or computer and an understanding of the term "hashtag."
3. An open mind, or the desire for one—the kind you had when you were four years old.
4. A desire for even one great wish to come true.
5. The reading list and the ability to set aside five to ten minutes a day.
6. The authors' website to get your free diploma, www.schoolofwishing.com.
7. A frame to hang your diploma!

Now you are ready. In this chapter alone, you will have what you need in order to get your degree in Wishing.

We are very serious wishers, authors, and people, and this course is not unlike who we are. We believe in this and think there is no harm in it, and like any course, it is our opinion, and it is not required that you agree with it, but if you do, then we hope you will enjoy this course and use it as a springboard to change the future, for better.

Preparation

In preparation for this course, the student must close his or her eyes (not yet) at the end of this paragraph. When eyes are closed, make a wish for anything at all. As soon as the wish is spoken (silently or not), open the eyes and the exercise is over. Try it now, and download the .pdf course if you like on the website www.schoolofwishing.com.

One minimum requirement for each day is to say a wish for someone else upon waking up or during the day. At the end of the day, choose a wish for yourself that you will stick with for every night for the period of eleven days, and after that you can choose a new wish or keep on repeating the same wish for an extra twenty days or until you feel it is enough. Sometimes you need to focus on wishes for longer to make them come true and sometimes you need to let them go for a while and then go back to them.

Course Overview—What to Expect

In the beginning of this course, we will guide you through daily routines until you are accustomed to the process of wishing every day. This process will continue throughout the whole eleven-day course as the readings begin on the third day. There are different books to read and you do not have to read all that is assigned, but the reading of other books in the course is meant to deepen your experience and personalize it in a way that is unique to you. There will be minor writing assignments to blog about wishes and share them at different points in the course. This is important and it is all designed to enable you to focus on wishes that can actually come true for several reasons, which range from the philosophical to the practical. The first two days do not require any reading, just a simple meditation and wishing.

We will now guide you through the process of wishing.

Day One

Look at the blog, or download the course if you would like to print it out—go to www.schoolofwishing.com to get it for free. If you are using paper, just get yourself prepared by finding a special pad and titling it "The School of Wishing Course."

Begin the day by making a wish just after you wake up. The morning wish must be for someone else—a wish for someone else's health, happiness, or anything at all.

Get comfortable in your wishing/meditation space. Sit up with your eyes closed and your palms on top of your thighs. Take a deep breath in through your nose, and exhale out through your mouth, and repeat. Continue focusing on your breathing throughout the whole process of making a wish. Breathe in: I need to let go of my fear. Breathe out: I am free of judgment. Breathe in: Say the wish for someone else. Breathe out: See it in your mind and feel it; smile while feeling the wish is becoming real. It is crystal clear what you are wishing for and you can experience the emotion of happiness while watching your wish come true in your mind.

You will repeat this exercise for the next eleven days upon waking. Remember, repetition helps to set the mind into a new paradigm, but repetition without feeling it is like doing something automatically without thinking, and that might not produce the desired effect. Before going to bed, on the first day, make a wish for yourself. Choose a wish that you will stick with every night for the period of eleven days, and after that you can choose a new wish or keep on repeating the same wish for an extra twenty days or until you feel it is enough, or until it comes true.

Lie down on your bed and close your eyes. Take a deep breath, in through your nose, and exhale out through your mouth. Repeat. Continue focusing on your breathing throughout the whole process of making a wish. Breathe in: I let go of all fear. Breathe out: I am free of judgment. Breathe in: Say your wish. Breathe out: See it in your mind and feel it; smile while feeling the wish is becoming real. It is crystal clear what you are wishing for and you can experience the emotion of happiness while watching your wish come true in your mind. Sweet dreams!

Day Two

On day two, you have figured out how to find our blog, and if you haven't, then you are following along right here and using paper and pen instead.

The exercise for day two is the same as day one, in a very brief moment, perhaps this one, or the one just after waking, close your eyes and make a wish for someone else. Close your eyes. Take a deep breath in through your nose and exhale out through your mouth. Repeat the breathing process. Continue focusing on your breathing throughout the whole process of making a wish. Breathe in: I am ready to let go of my fear. Breathe out: I am brave. Breathe in: Say the wish for someone else. Breathe out: See it in your mind and feel it; smile while feeling the wish is becoming real. It is crystal clear what you are wishing for and you can experience the emotion of happiness while watching your wish come true in your mind.

Then open your eyes, and you are done. Pat yourself on the back, day two is over and you are already on the way to becoming an experienced practitioner! The idea is to have fun with this. It is a course that requires some work, but start easily, so you are inspired. Take your time—there is no need to rush—even one wish a day is very powerful work.

Before you fall asleep lying on your bed, close your eyes. Take a deep breath in through your nose and exhale out through your mouth and repeat. Continue focusing on your breathing throughout the whole process of making a wish. Breathe in: I am ready to let go of my fear. Breathe out: I am brave. Breathe in: Say your wish. Breathe out: See it in your mind, feel it, and smile while feeling the wish is becoming real. It is crystal clear what you are wishing for and you can experience the emotion of happiness while watching your wish come true in your mind.

Day Three

After rising from sleep, as soon as possible, make a wish for someone else, anyone at all, even if you don't know them. Get comfortable in your wishing/meditation space. Sit up with your eyes closed and your palms on top of your thighs. Take a deep breath in through your nose and exhale out through your mouth and repeat. Continue focusing on your breathing throughout the whole process of making a wish. Breathe in: I want to let go of my fear. Breathe out: I shall receive. Breathe in: Say the wish for someone else. Breathe out: See it in your mind and feel it; smile while feeling the wish is becoming real. It is crystal clear what you are wishing for and you can experience the emotion of happiness while watching your wish come true in your mind.

We will begin the reading today, and also discuss the idea of wishing for others, as well as ourselves, as a type of inter-

personal exchange. A smile for a smile, for example, seems natural, and making a wish for someone else, and that wish being returned, also feels natural to us.

The book we will start reading is *The Ingenious Gentleman Don Quixote of La Mancha*, by Miguel de Cervantes. The introduction should be read as well as the first five chapters, which are all rather short.

This text was chosen because it is a great pleasure to read, and also because it will give us a nontheological perspective on what it means to wish for something that is impossible to attain.

At the end of day three, lie down on your bed and close your eyes. Take a deep breath in through your nose and exhale out through your mouth. Do this twice. Continue focusing on your breathing throughout the whole process of making a wish. Breathe in: I want to let go of my fear. Breathe out: I shall receive. Breathe in: Say your wish. Breathe out: See it in your mind and feel it; smile while feeling the wish is becoming real. It is crystal clear what you are wishing for and you can experience the emotion of happiness while watching your wish come true in your mind.

We will discuss the life of Miguel de Cervantes as well as the selected chapters, but first read them so that you can know the pleasure of reading one of the great masterworks of literature. In Spanish it is of course even better, but Miguel de Cervantes is a contemporary of Shakespeare and has all the brilliance of a mind like Shakespeare. Don Quixote still has a contemporary ring to it and is a postmodern book in many ways because the book often refers to itself, in a very funny way, and how it is being written, so there are several layers to the narrative that feel modern.

Miguel de Cervantes Was a Hero

Before thinking about the story, it would help to know some things about the author who lived in sixteenth-century Spain. Miguel de Cervantes lived at a time when novels of Knight-Errantry, or stories about knights doing good deeds in shining armor, were the pulp fiction of the day. Everyone loved to read them, but the books were also looked down upon by intellectuals as well as the church, because the writing, with all the romance and impossible adventures, was thought to border on heresy. Nevertheless, it was tolerated and the market for stories about gallant knights in armor continued to grow.

Cervantes's book, *Don Quixote*, is a critique on that genre of book, and was an inside joke at the time, thus you would understand the references to current books about knights if you were living then. Today, the equivalent might be vampire or wizard novels for young adults, a market that is rapidly growing.

The main character, Don Quixote, is a lord from a small town in Spain. He loves books of chivalry, stories about the lives of gallant knights, and begins to devour as many as he can, reading night and day.

After many weeks of reading, he develops a type of insanity. That is, he becomes insane, or at least delusional, because he has read so many books. The characters in the books become real to him, and it is as if he knows them, because he has read so much about them. Don Quixote decides in his madness to become a traveling knight himself and find a squire to accompany him as well as a woman to whom he may pledge his heart and deeds. He believes that books of knights-errant are true stories and he has become inspired to set out on his own adventure. His madness is that he believes fiction to be real and goes out into the world assuming it is all true, and that he is a real knight himself.

Quixote, Quixotic: The Modern Novel

The book is comical from the start. A man, a fool really, has read so much he believes his books of fiction are real and is out to replicate life as told in the books. Doesn't that sound like a modern novel? It is the book that opened the door for many writers to experiment with the form of the novel. As his adventures begin, we can see how funny, as well as how deeply delusional, Don Quixote is.

He has made a very real wish to change his life. Don Quixote has based his wish on books that he believed were real. So real that he is modeling his daily activities on them and has made them his life's work. There are many interpretations of this great book, and many revolve around the idea of Don Quixote as a man, pursuing his dreams, but he is also

a man who is wishing and gambling with his life. He makes himself a lance and a helmet out of household items before mounting his horse with his squire, Sancho Panza, who rides on a donkey.

It is a joke to the reader, but not to Don Quixote who believes in everything he is doing.

Those who wish and those who dream, especially out loud in public, face ridicule as the possible outcome of wishes that failed to come true. To make a wish as grand as Don Quixote's, and pursue that wish no matter how insane, is not the model we may want to follow, but isn't it similar to pursuing your business or artistic dream when the odds are slim?

On the blog at www.schoolofwishing.com start a post about this. Do you know a story where someone has pursued a wish or a dream that seemed entirely ridiculous, only to succeed in the end?

As you read the book, stop after chapter three, sit back, reflect a little and join the classroom discussion about what Don Quixote is doing and what it means to pursue a wish even if it seems crazy. Share a story about something that you know that happened against the odds. It could be a paragraph or longer.

Being a Good Christian Soldier in the 1600s

As you continue to read on to chapter four, you might see a touch of a morality tale. The author, Cervantes, was a good Christian soldier in real life, and he was well aware that books about chivalry were looked down upon. He also knew that for any book to be published, it had to go through the church censors first, so he had to keep ideas from veering into the realm of heresy or something similar. Oddly, the current *Harry Potter* series is similar. Some churches and conservative groups denounced the series because it encourages a belief in the occult, magic, witches, and wizards, all historically heretical subjects. That may seem old-fashioned now, but the same ideas of what is real, potentially, and what is not, continue to engage us. We want to know if dreams really can come true, and if so, the recipe to get there. Is there magic to be made or conjured? Can an improbable journey end up being a success without any preparation?

To the author's credit, a decision is not really cast as to whether Don Quixote is successful or not. He is viewed with humor and admiration, but the reader is also wondering at what moment this insanity will explode or implode.

For the next piece of writing on the blog or your pad, we would like you to prepare a story about something you have done, or someone else has done, that seemed foolish perhaps, but turned out to be heroic—an act that seemed silly or worse, but was redeemed somehow by the end result. If you can't think of one, choose one from a movie or book.

The Fool

Perhaps there is a movie or television show or YouTube video you have seen where the main character does something crazy to pursue his wish or desire, which makes him or her look ridiculous, yet receives the admiration of friends in the end. This is a story that keeps repeating itself and deserves to be examined here.

To prepare your writing, use a separate piece of paper or digital document on your computer or phone, or the blog, www.schoolofwishing.com, and tell the story in three hundred words or less. You are not writing a polished piece, but make it something clear and easy to understand. Begin the piece of writing by explaining what you are going to tell us about, then write, and wrap up the writing with a summary or conclusion that reiterates your stated goal at the beginning of the writing.

When you are done, post it on the blog, www.school-ofwishing.com, in the section called "Day 3 Stories" or use that line in your post title.

The brief version of this part of the course: make a wish for someone else before you go to sleep. Also always try to remember to smile as soon as you wake up and before you fall asleep. Even if you don't feel like it, force yourself to smile while thinking of your wish becoming a reality.

Day Four

Begin the day wishing for someone else, just after waking. Get comfortable in your wishing/meditation space. Sit up with your eyes closed and your palms on top of your thighs. Take a deep breath in through your nose and exhale out through your mouth, and do this twice. Continue focusing on your breath throughout the whole process of making a wish. Breathe in: I have courage. Breathe out: I am free of fear. Breathe in: Say the wish for someone else. Breathe out: See it in your mind, feel it, and smile while the wish is becoming real. It is crystal clear what you are wishing for and you can experience the emotion of happiness while watching your wish come true in your mind.

Hopefully you enjoyed reading *Don Quixote*; you should be getting a few laughs out of it! You don't have to stay on this strict schedule, just move on to the next day when you are done with your reading. If you don't want to do the reading, then be sure to make at least one wish a day for someone else.

The final discussion is about his adventures and what, if anything, they represent.

Our main character, Don Quixote, is out for the first time to achieve his wish, his desire to be a gallant knight. His first encounter illustrates the level of his delusion. He is riding along with his squire and sees huge windmills slowly spinning. In his mind, the windmills are giants that are about to attack. Even though his squire explains that they are in fact windmills, Quixote refuses to believe it. With his lance in his hand, he charges at the windmill to defeat it. He is quickly and powerfully thrown to the ground sustaining serious injuries. He does not feel defeated. On the contrary, he feels that he has accomplished something in his first battle. He

knows that the giants look like windmills, but he sees that as evidence that the giants have transformed themselves to look like windmills to fool him.

There is nothing his squire can say to make him change his mind. After resting and recovering a bit, they travel on in search of another "adventure," feeling sore, hungry, and thirsty. This is the pattern for much of the rest of the book; an adventure begins, Don Quixote never waivers from his goal, and gets nearly killed and in all kinds of trouble as well!

What do these adventures mean to you? What do you think they represent?

Learning is writing, so your homework is to do some on the blog, www.schoolofwishing.com.

Answer the questions above or comment on any other aspect of Don Quixote's life and what wishing brings to mind in this context. Or just comment and enter any conversation there.

At the end of day four, lie down on your bed, close your eyes. Take a deep breath in through your nose and exhale out through your mouth. Do this twice. Continue focusing on your breathing throughout the whole process of making a wish. Breathe in: I am free of fear. Breathe out: I have courage. Breathe in: Say your wish. Breathe out: See it in your mind and feel it; smile while feeling the wish is becoming real. It is crystal clear what you are wishing for and you can experience the emotion of happiness while watching your wish come true in your mind.

Day Five

Begin this day, like all days, after waking, make a wish that is for someone else. Get comfortable in your wishing/meditation space. Sit up with your eyes closed and your palms on top of your thighs. Take a deep breath in through your nose and exhale out through your mouth, and do this twice. Continue focusing on your breathing throughout the whole process of making a wish. Breathe in: I will not judge. Breathe out: I have no fear therefore I shall receive. Breathe in: Say the wish for someone else. Breathe out: See it in your mind and feel it; smile while feeling the wish is becoming real. It is crystal clear what you are wishing for and you can experience the emotion of happiness while watching your wish come true in your mind.

If you thought *Don Quixote* was difficult, then Freud will be even more so! But it will also be a very rewarding read.

Begin reading the text of Freud's classic, *The Interpretation of Dreams.*

At the end of this day after your reading, lie down on your bed and close your eyes. Take a deep breath in through your nose and exhale out through your mouth, and do this twice. Continue focusing on your breathing throughout the whole process of making a wish. Breathe in: I will not judge. Breathe out: I have no fear therefore I shall receive. Breathe in: Say your wish. Breathe out: See it in your mind and feel it; smile while feeling the wish is becoming real. It is crystal clear what you are wishing for and you can experience the emotion of happiness while watching your wish come true in your mind.

Read the preface and skip to chapter three: "A Dream Is the Fulfillment of a Wish." Freud takes a bit of interpreting to understand.

When Freud was writing this now classic book, *The Interpretation of Dreams*, he was spending the summer of 1895 at manor Belle Vue, near Grinzing in Austria. On June 12th, 1900, he wrote a letter to Wilhelm Fliess, saying, "Do you suppose that some day a marble tablet will be placed on the house, inscribed with these words: 'In this house on July 24th, 1895, the secret of dreams was revealed to Dr. Sigm. Freud'? At the moment I see little prospect of it."

The Wish Realized

In 1963, Belle Vue manor was demolished, but today a memorial plaque with just an inscription of that quote has been erected at the site by the Sigmund Freud Society of Austria.

It is an ironic footnote of wish fulfillment theory that his thought came true. It is a curious twist. Did that memorial plaque get installed because of the letter, his wish? In this case it looks like that was exactly the reason, but it is impossible to say for sure. His fans erected that because of that piece of writing, as well as his achievements. Freud's wish, in a sense, was written down, given a voice, and thus it was possible for another person or persons to fulfill it, which they did.

Let's look at what the term "wish fulfillment" actually means.

Freud believed that the dreams we have are the results of what we wish for.

His theory, in part, was that the dream was fulfilling the wish that had not yet been realized.

If we wish to have a dog, for example, we might have a dream of owning a dog. Therefore, by analyzing a patient's dreams, he could decipher what wishes were being fulfilled by working backwards from the dream. It's a fantastic idea—we don't know what we really want, or wish for, but our dreams can tell us.

Not Knowing What We Wish For

We may not know what we are consciously wishing for, but if our dreams are the projections of those wishes, then that is the only example we need—to look in the narrative of the dream and see beneath the surface, what we didn't know we were wishing for.

Perhaps this is a type of "alignment," coined many years after Freud. Let's say we analyze all our dreams, and come to an understanding of who we are based on the wishes we are decoding through regular Freudian therapy sessions. Let's say you have been going to Freudian therapy sessions for several years and you are comfortable now, or at least more so, with the unconscious wishes you are always making that keep bubbling to the surface. You still have questions, but your basic understanding of your own wishes through regular dream interpretation is clear, or becoming so. Whether you act on those wishes or not, you know what they are. Of course you are probably not undergoing Freudian analysis, but you can often remember your dreams.

This is a really interesting way of looking at how dreams and the role of wishes work in wish fulfillment—as powerful guides in our conscious and unconscious lives every day. We are making up new wishes all day long, and most of these wishes we are not aware of and thus we are not making an effort to achieve or actualize them in any way. Like a sculptor revealing the figure within the stone, we have wishes that are there, waiting to be revealed. Our dreams can reveal those wishes to us.

Share Your Dreams

In the next few days, we are going to be talking and blogging about dreams. So try to put a note on your computer or phone, with an alarm, to wake you in the morning and prompt you to write down what you remember from a dream. You might think you don't have dreams because you haven't thought it about it for a while. Well, if you begin to practice writing down your dreams, you will get better at it, and the process of remembering will be activated again.

It is interesting how we can turn off our recollection of dreams if we want to. It seems most people can and do willfully turn off their ability to remember dreams. But since they are created by the unconscious mind, dreams never stop occurring, and they can be retrieved. Dreams are generated all the time. During the day they are generated, and at night they are generated.

To gather your dreams, just begin to wake up to an alarm, write something, and even go back to sleep after that. But to begin with, if you wake yourself up with the intention of writing a sentence or two about a dream, it will begin to work. After a few days of waking up and writing something about a dream, a story will emerge, however fractured. With simple practice, like any art, you will begin to remember more and more.

Write down some dreams on the www.schoolofwishing. com blog, if they can be shared, and keep reading other peoples' dreams on the blog. You are entering a community of dreamers who are tracking their dreams for different reasons. For the purpose of this course, and of this book, we are tracking dreams to uncover the wishes underneath.

If Freud is right, and dreams are the product of wish fulfillment, then they are the best way to access the wishes that come from our greatest desires, unknown even to ourselves.

In this section of the course, you are trying to uncover a wish of your own that you didn't know you had. Don't go on

to the next chapter if possible without completing this step and writing down at least three dreams.

It's simple really. Set an alarm to go off early in the morning, and with a pad and pencil or smartphone note pad app nearby, write a sentence about any dream you can remember. Do that for five days and see what happens. If you remember anything at all, you are ready to go to the next step.

Always Remember Your Dreams, Literally

A friend of ours is a Freudian therapist who is retired. We asked him what he thought constituted "success" in the treatment of a patient. That is, if someone has been going to therapy for years, decades even, is there a sign that they no longer need therapy?

He felt that if a patient regularly woke each morning, remembered and wrote down his or her dreams, and analyzed them on the spot, they would be very evolved, so to speak. A mark of Freudian therapy mastery, to some degree, is seen as a person who can regularly use their own dreams to understand their unconscious wishes and motives.

This part of the course could be the most beneficial for some, because it can be an ongoing or infrequent process with profound effects. To write down your dreams regularly has many other benefits, even if you don't analyze them. You may not be a writer, but when you do see stories coming from your mind on a regular basis, it does something to you. You are being creative even if it seems you are just a journalist of your own mind. In fact, you also created the news, so it is all your art, if it is your dream that is being written down.

Wish Fulfillment

The stories in your dreams may be thought-provoking on their own, without analysis. Certainly not all dreams are wish fulfillment, but most have an interesting narrative, or lack of narrative, as if they were time portals, because the normal rules of reality do not apply. So when you write down your dreams and you see all the things you create in your mind, it fills you with the joy of the "creator," which is simply the feeling of creating something unique, the way an artist does. It is an added benefit, a kind of small euphoria in this process. Your dreams are your art, and the more you see all the art you are making, the more you understand yourself. Writing down dreams is essential; otherwise they are forgotten because they are treated as unnecessary.

Dreaming, for wish fulfillment or not, is truly another world. Though we know little about the mind in terms of unconscious thoughts and impulses, we can see that at night our mind enters a type of surrealistic territory. Dream imagery was popular with the surrealists leading to the cliché idea of a dream being "surreal" today. Salvador Dalí and other surrealists seem to have been exploring ideas of other realities, the dream being only one example. Artists are always trying to learn more about themselves and their world, so this is another reason why using your dreams is part of the material you need to know yourself better, and to allow your wishes to come true, and to be creative in general.

Allowing Wishes

Allowing your wishes to come true, in this case, might mean not getting in the way of them. Because of self-worth issues, which nearly everyone has on different levels, our ambitions are held back by no one other than ourselves. We can all sabotage ourselves in matters of business or personal relationships, and only we know we did it. It is human to do so, but if we are to stop self-sabotaging, then we need to know what the wish is that we keep preventing ourselves from attaining.

That is a profound notion if taken seriously. The one obstacle we can often never surmount is the knowledge of our own self-limits. No matter what the reason, we all set certain limits on what we can achieve, but those limits can also be changed if we make a conscious effort. In the interpretation of your own dreams, or at least the attempt of this act, there is the possibility of reprogramming yourself to align more easily with the wish you want.

If you never knew your greatest wish was to travel to Alaska, how can you expect to ever get there? The good news is that all our wishes are waiting for us, right now, in our unconscious minds.

In the case of guilt or conflict influencing a dream, it can get much more complex and difficult to weed out your wishes, thus your effort to interpret and practice as much as possible is crucial.

From the beginning of *The Interpretation of Dreams*, Freud writes:

> In the following pages, I shall demonstrate that there exists a psychological technique by which dreams may be interpreted and that upon the application of this method every dream will show itself to be a senseful psychological structure which may be introduced into an assignable place in the psychic activity of the waking state.

It seems simple enough at first, but these "assignable places" where we put the conclusions we draw from our dreams is in the waking state. During the day, in other words, the pieces of the puzzle that our dreams reveal about our wishes will resolve daily conflicts if placed correctly. You can pursue your wishes consciously. This process of writing down your dreams is of the utmost importance and the most powerful part of this course in terms of physiological and psychological changes in your being. Because if you can even begin to decode your dreams of wish fulfillment, you have completed a very important step. Deducing your greatest wish from that self-decoding process can be a guiding light in your life. Isn't that the ideal goal of Freudian therapy as well as the goal of this book? Knowing our wishes adds purpose and guidance to our lives.

Dreamers

If we could all wake up every day, remember our dreams, decode them, and understand our wishes, we would be better for it and closer to seeing those wishes come true.

The same can be done during the day. We are having minor daydreams all the time, and as we walk through our day, our mind is going all over the place. Perhaps we are seeing advertisements and we begin to want or wish for this or that. Or perhaps we are unconsciously thinking about a place we want to go or a person we want to meet. These are all dreams for things we want during the day. With practice, as we understand our sleeping dreams, we can become more aware of our daydreams and learn to be guided by them, or at least to pause and reflect on what they mean.

On the blog, www.schoolofwishing.com, you can contribute to the conversation by posting in one of the categories, and seeing what others are saying. The more we write and share our dreams, the better chances we have at getting our wish revealed so that it can come true in the waking world.

Day Six

Begin the day by making a wish for someone else. Get comfortable in your wishing/meditation space. Sit up with your eyes closed and your palms on top of your thighs. Take a

deep breath in through your nose and exhale out through your mouth, and do this twice. Continue focusing on your breathing throughout the whole process of making a wish. Breathe in: Asking will bring me closer to my wish. Breathe out: I am ready to receive. Breathe in: Say the wish for someone else. Breathe out: See it in your mind and feel it; smile while feeling the wish is becoming real. It is crystal clear what you are wishing for and you can experience the emotion of happiness while watching your wish come true in your mind.

Before bed, make a new wish. Lie down on your bed and close your eyes. Take a deep breath in through your nose and exhale out through your mouth, and do this twice. Continue focusing on your breathing throughout the whole process of making a wish. Breathe in: Asking will bring me closer to my wish. Breathe out: I am ready to receive. Breathe in: Say your wish. Breathe out: See it in your mind and feel it; smile while feeling the wish is becoming real. It is crystal clear what you are wishing for and you can experience the emotion of happiness while watching your wish come true in your mind.

After you spend a few days reading over Freud's book, *The Interpretation of Dreams*, you can continue the process of writing down your dreams every morning while moving on to the next text, if you are enjoying the process.

A Course in Miracles

A Course in Miracles is the next book from which to read selections. We think *A Course in Miracles* is a very unusual book that deserves more attention.

Begin by reading the preface and then start the first exercise, which will take five minutes and is a meditation for one day. For the purpose of this course, we are doing the first exercise. It will take five days for this one exercise to be completed unless you want to do only the first day of reading, and make it one day. If you take five days for this, repeat the special daily wishes at the beginning of this chapter (page 116) for every day, otherwise move on after one day.

These are exercises and meditations that will be very easy to undertake and each will take less than a minute to do. However, we think you will find that the meditations are geared toward changing your entire way of seeing the world.

The preface is an important text to read here because it explains how the book was written, which is highly unusual and is something of a miracle in itself. The author talks about writing down her dreams, which were very symbolic, and she also says she was receiving a type of inner dictation, not an audible voice, that she wrote down in shorthand. The first words of the course she wrote were "This is a Course in Miracles."

A Voice

We have never read anything like the preface in *A Course in Miracles*. It is a highly unusual piece of writing. It is an explanation of a miracle, really. Most people write a book by outlining its contents and filling in the chapters, but this is a book that was written through an inner voice. If it were being examined and evaluated to determine if a real miracle took place here, it might pass the test. We could say we have character witnesses for the author, who was a working professor of psychology at Columbia, and we have many people around her at that time who are still alive and are well respected in their fields. If there ever was a modern case for a miracle, this is it. It is a giant book of highly spiritual writing at the very least, and even though we are just dipping into it for the purpose of this wishing course, it could be read in its entirety if you are inclined, because it is a teaching device that is well planned and easy to use. If this book is miraculous in its creation, then it also came from a wish. In the preface you will read that as a result of frustration, two psychologists wished there was another way to communicate and work with people, and from that desire came the unusual story of the book's writing process.

After you read the preface, move on to the very brief introduction and the first chapter. The introduction, which is less than half a page, is the beginning of the book and sets the tone for its program. It is a course in miracles, and it is designed to teach. The introduction clarifies that it will not teach what love means, but it will strive to remove the blocks that are in the way to understanding love's presence. It goes on to say that "The opposite of love is fear, but what is all-encompassing can have no opposite."

The most powerful and enigmatic lines of the book are the last of the introduction. To sum up the entire book, the following words are used: "Nothing real can be threatened. Nothing unreal exists."

After reading the introduction, pause a bit and reflect on what that means before moving on to the first chapter. If you want to, you can also go to the blog, www.schoolofwishing.com and write something there about your thoughts after reading the preface and first chapter.

When the course says, "nothing real can be threatened," it is talking about the presence of love, which is a very powerful idea. If love is truly the only thing that is real in this world, and fear is its opposite, then this course teaches you that there is never anything to fear and the only thing that surrounds you is love. This is a very radical idea because it upends everything we think we know.

Fear in the World

It seems as though the world is full of fears, and that there is no way around them.

Fear of sickness, fear of death, fear of loss, and the list goes on. This course is saying that the love that surrounds you and comes from inside you cannot be threatened in any way. This is a concept that we generally don't believe in, because we are taught daily that we are surrounded by fears that can in fact change our lives at any minute. But *A Course in Miracles* goes further by saying, "nothing unreal exists." That would mean that anything that is not love is also not real. Here is another idea that seems impossible to believe. Sickness and death are not real? A broken arm is not real? According to the book, no, those things are not real. But don't get defensive yet, though that is expected, because there is a deeper meaning here and a new meaning to what "real" actually means. Something real is something that can truly threaten us, thus the common fear of sickness and death. According to the book, these things do not exist, not because people do not get sick and die, but because we are seeing them incorrectly. We use fears like sickness and loss to deny the possibilities of miracles and love. If we think that material loss and loss of our health are more powerful than any miracle or love, we have built a case to deny the existence of an all-encompassing love or the possibility of a miracle. We cannot believe both things at the same time. It is a confusing concept because we are now programmed to believe that this idea is impossible. Can love truly conquer all? This is the question that is more or less answered by the section we are about to read. The goal is to see how this line of thinking could develop and help with the idea of wish fulfillment or wishes coming true.

Miracles

After you read the preface and introduction, which are both very short, read only pages 3–6 of chapter one, "The Meaning of Miracles."

It is a laundry list about what a miracle is and is not, but it will also introduce you to how this book is being written and we think it is an inspiring few pages. While this may or may not sound very Christian-based to you, it is not. This is not a book that is embraced by the Catholic Church because it goes too far into what seems like Eastern thinking, and it is not a book that is embraced easily by Eastern gurus and thinkers because it feels too Western. In fact, the book is trying to teach the same thing that almost all religions are after—true peace of mind, or at least the pursuit of peace.

Nothing I See Means Anything

After reading the preface, introduction, and the first few pages of chapter one, let's move on to the workbook. The workbook has a brief introduction, and then begins the first lesson of the workbook, which is titled, "Nothing I see in this room (on this street, from this window, in this place) means anything."

Read and do that exercise and see how it feels. It is the beginning of the process to undo almost everything you know. It is reorienting your outlook to question everything and see what is happening as unreal. As difficult as this may be to understand, be clear that the goal here is peace of mind. Besides decreasing your fears, it will also teach you how to perform miracles.

In the next day or week, spend the few minutes required a day to complete lessons one through seven. This may be the most powerful part of this course for you, but either way it is meant to be a launching point for your own process of wishing for what you want and making a miracle happen. Record your thoughts on this section of the course at www.schoolofwishing.com.

A Course in Miracles is in one way just another book, but like all the books on this reading list, it has had a profound impact on a tremendous number of people for a reason. It is not a self-help book on how to be happier or how to live a better life; it is a powerful spiritual text that is meant to give you peace of mind and teach you to be a miracle worker.

Day Seven

Begin the day after waking up by making a wish for someone else, anyone at all. Get comfortable in your wishing/meditation space. Sit up with your eyes closed and your palms on top of your thighs. Take a deep breath in through your nose and exhale out through your mouth. Do this twice. Continue focusing on your breathing throughout the whole process of making a wish. Breathe in: I am love. Breathe out: Love helps me achieve my wish. Breathe in: Say the wish for someone else. Breathe out: See it in your mind and feel it; smile while feeling the wish is becoming real. It is crystal clear what you are wishing for and you can experience the emotion of happiness while watching your wish come true in your mind.

Before you fall asleep in your bed, lie down and close your eyes. Take a deep breath in through your nose and exhale out through your mouth, and do this twice. Continue focusing on your breathing throughout the whole process of making a wish. Breathe in: I am love. Breathe out: Love helps me achieve my wish. Breathe in: Say your wish. Breathe out: See it in your mind and feel it; smile while feeling the wish is becoming real. It is crystal clear what you are wishing for and you can experience the emotion of happiness while watching your wish come true in your mind.

Next on the reading list is *I Am That,* a transcription of talks and commentary of Sri Nisargadatta Maharaj, a guru who by all deeds and words seems to be authentic. His words are extremely profound to many people, and this book has been called a "modern spiritual classic." He died in 1981 at the age of eighty-three.

This book sounds strikingly similar to *A Course in Miracles*. In so many powerful spiritual guidebooks or "classics," there is often a common goal, a similar state of mind. This is an example. Before we even start reading this book, please note something the guru said in the early 1970s, a phrase that was published before the book was written, which is considered one of his most profound thoughts: "The real does not die, the unreal never lived."

A Course in Miracles said, "nothing real can be threatened, nothing unreal exists."

The similarity of these two exceptional statements points toward the truth of this enigmatic phrase which we will explore more now through this text.

I Am That

Begin by reading the introductory texts and the editor's note to *I Am That*, because collectively it gives you the sense of this guru as an authentic intellectual who might be enlightened. That is a lot to say about anyone. Jesus was presumably enlightened, or close to it, as was Buddha and perhaps many of the saints. It is a rare trait, as we know it. *A Course in Miracles* is written from an enlightened point of view, it seems. Like the book *I Am That*, there is tremendous conviction and certainty behind the words, as would befit a great or nearly enlightened teacher.

It seems no coincidence then, that the words from two sources that should both be considered "spiritual classics," are so similar. Enlightenment, or at least an evolved sense of who we are, is sought after in both of these books, and both are written as though the teacher is a great sage with little or no ego at all, making the case even more convincing that these are truly great teachers. *I Am That* is a series of interviews with a great teacher or guru. *A Course in Miracles* is written in the first person with the voice of a humble yet powerful prophet.

The guru said, "The real does not die, the unreal never lived." *A Course in Miracles* said, "nothing real can be threatened, nothing unreal exists."

Both books say the "unreal does not exist." Why would that have to be written and singled out as such an important phrase? Isn't that obvious?

In *I Am That*, the guru is saying that the only thing that is real is the *awareness* of our mind and body itself. Neither the mind nor the body is real because we are not that, but we are the state of *witnessing that*. Furthermore, this state of being aware of our body and mind and watching them both like an observer existed prior to our being, before our mind and memory itself. It is like a collective force that is at once outside us and inside us. It could also be called "our original essence," or our "natural inheritance," as *A Course in Miracles* calls it. Other names could be the *True Self*, which in Hinduism is also called the *Atman*. Whatever you call it, it is the idea of an observer, a witness, which is ultimately what is real. Everything else is not real.

What Is Real?

There are a few ways of learning and really understanding the above phrase, because most people cannot easily believe that, but it has the ring of truth to it. If there were only a bridge to more easily access this notion . . . That is what *A Course in Miracles* is, a teaching source to get you there, and so is the book *I Am That*. Both books are designed for the seeker who may want to teach, because the other way of learning this is to just believe it.

Since it is not intuitive and requires you to let go of some notions of what is real, it is difficult for some people, as it should be. The other method, because all are not leaders or intellectuals, is to learn it by doing it, not necessarily understanding it. If you choose for example not to pursue the understanding of this "witness of yourself" idea as the only real thing, but if you still think it might be true, you can do the physical work instead, that is, follow until you understand. That is in fact the role of a disciple-guru relationship, which does not exist in the West in the way it did and still does in the East. But the guru interviewed in *I Am That*, Sri Nisargadatta Maharaj, jokes about his own guru saying, "my Guru ordered me to attend to the sense 'I am' and to give attention to nothing else. I just obeyed. I did not follow any particular course of breathing, or meditation, or study of scriptures. Whatever happened, I would turn away my attention from it and remain with the sense 'I am.' It may look too simple, even crude. My only reason for doing it was that my guru told me so. Yet it worked!"

The Guru

That is a learning method we know little of in the West, that is, the idea of just saying "Do this" because the teacher says so, not because you understand why. Even if you do grasp abstract concepts like this, following a series of ideas or meditations can help the seeker to find a state of being more easily than just trying to understand it. This book will help with understanding, and *A Course in Miracles* is one path to doing it because the book has clear instructions. In other words, following a course of exercise, as outlined there, is another path to get you to the same state of mind, so if you are looking for *what to do* instead of *why*, then follow all the exercises of meditation in *A Course in Miracles*. Continue reading *I Am That* as well for more understanding of these abstract concepts and use the blog www.schoolofwishing. com to share or discuss *I Am That* with others.

Day Eight

Begin the day as always: after waking up, make a wish for someone else. It could be for health, happiness, or anything at all. Get comfortable in your wishing/meditation space. Sit up with your eyes closed and your palms on top of your thighs. Take a deep breath in through your nose and exhale out through your mouth. Do this twice. Continue focusing on your breathing throughout the whole process of making a wish. Breathe in: I am brave to ask. Breathe out: I am free to receive. Breathe in: Say the wish for someone else. Breathe out: See it in your mind and feel it; smile while feeling the wish is becoming real. It is crystal clear what you are wishing for and you can experience the emotion of happiness while watching your wish come true in your mind.

Before you fall asleep in your bed, close your eyes. Take a deep breath in through your nose and exhale out through your mouth, and do this twice. Continue focusing on your breathing throughout the whole process of making a wish. Breathe in: I am brave to ask. Breathe out: I am free to receive. Breathe in: Say your wish. Breathe out: See it in your mind and feel it; smile while feeling the wish is becoming real. It is crystal clear what you are wishing for and you can experience the emotion of happiness while watching your wish come true in your mind

Read the *Autobiography of a Yogi*—the introduction and first chapter. You can get this online for free in many places, or your local library.

Here is another very Eastern story written by a well-known guru, Paramahansa Yogananda, who died in 1952. This story was first published in 1946. Like the other books we are reading here, it is considered a "spiritual classic" and tells the early life of a guru and how he spread his teaching all across the West. He explains the process of looking for a guru of his own and calmly describes being in two places at once as well as other phenomena not usually written about. This was one of the favorite books of the late Steve Jobs, founder of Apple Inc., who was also a visionary. He deeply admired this book and said that he read it every year. The late George Harrison of the Beatles also thought it was a pivotal text and gave it to friends, and the list goes on of major figures who were influenced by this essential text. The book is full of the miraculous—to some people, too much so. It is hard to believe what is being said, and it is being introduced here because like the previous books we have been reading, it points to a life experience that is radically different from our own yet accessible at the same time.

After reading the introduction and first chapter, reflect on his early life and how that set the stage for him. What concepts here feel similar to yours or different? Write down your thoughts on the schoolofwishing.com blog or on your paper.

Day Nine

Begin the day by making a wish for someone else. Get comfortable in your wishing/meditation space. Sit up with your eyes closed and your palms on top of your thighs. Take a deep breath in through your nose and exhale out through your mouth, and do this twice. Continue focusing on your breathing throughout the whole process of making a wish. Breathe in: I believe in miracles. Breathe out: Miracles are as natural as being. Breathe in: Say the wish for someone else. Breathe out: See it in your mind and feel it; smile while feeling the wish is becoming real. It is crystal clear what you are wishing for and you can experience the emotion of happiness while watching your wish come true in your mind.

End the day, just before going to bed, with a wish. Before you fall asleep lying in your bed, close your eyes. Take a deep breath in through your nose and exhale out through your mouth, and do this twice. Continue focusing on your breathing throughout the whole process of making a wish. Breathe in: I believe in miracles. Breathe out: Miracles are as natural as being. Breathe in: Say your wish. Breathe out: See it in your mind and feel it; smile while feeling the wish is becoming real. It is crystal clear what you are wishing for and you can experience the emotion of happiness while watching your wish come true in your mind.

The *Tao Te Ching* was written in approximately the sixth century BC by Lao Tzu. It is a book of poems that has influenced a great deal of religious thinking in the East since then. There are many translations, but it is a public domain book now with numerous free editions as well as beautifully crafted new editions. It is eighty-one short poems and a very easy read. Try reading the first five poems. They are some-

what enigmatic, prone to endless translations, and have different meanings for everyone. Consider this example:

In Tao the only motion is returning;
The only useful quality, weakness.
For though all creatures under heaven are the products
of Being,
Being itself is the product of Not-being.
(chap. 40, tr. Waley)

Enjoy reading this book and take your time before moving on to the next book, and share your thoughts with others on this.

Day Ten

Begin the day by making a wish just after waking. As with every day in this course, the wish in the morning is for someone else. Get comfortable in your wishing/meditation space. Sit up with your eyes closed and your palms on top of your thighs. Take a deep breath in through your nose and exhale out through your mouth, and do this twice. Continue focusing on your breathing throughout the whole process of making a wish. Breathe in: I am ready to manifest. Breathe out: Miracles are all around me. Breathe in: Say the wish for someone else. Breathe out: See it in your mind and feel it; smile while feeling the wish is becoming real. It is crystal clear what you are wishing for and you can experience the emotion of happiness while watching your wish come true in your mind.

End the day by making your wish. Before you fall asleep lying in your bed, close your eyes. Take a deep breath in through your nose and exhale out through your mouth, and do this twice. Continue focusing on your breathing throughout the whole process of making a wish. Breathe in: I am ready to manifest. Breathe out: Miracles are all around me. Breathe in: Say your wish. Breathe out: See it in your mind and feel it; smile while feeling the wish is becoming real. It is crystal clear what you are wishing for and you can experience the emotion of happiness while watching your wish come true in your mind.

The Book of Job, New Testament, The Bible

We discussed the book of Job and his incredible story earlier in this book. It is an epic poem, not a difficult read, so find a translation that makes sense to you and is readable. There are many modern translations to look through and choose from, we prefer the Jerusalem Bible for its ease of reading, but there are many. Just find one that is not in language so archaic that it makes no sense, but sounds pretty, like the King James translation.

Read the beginning so you can understand the deal that was made between God and Satan, and stop when Job begins to curse his situation. This is an incredibly powerful text about the opposite of wishing for things or using medita-

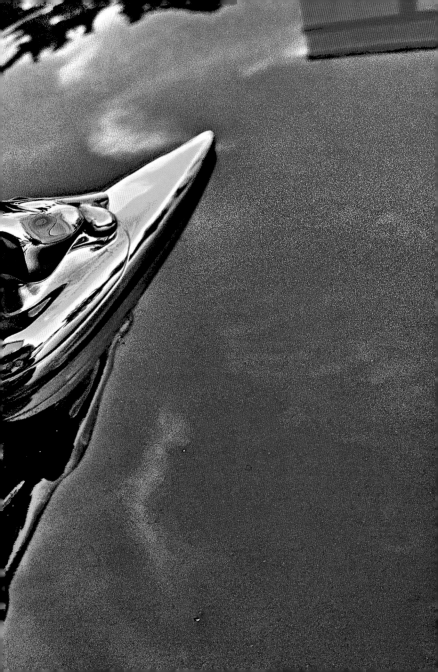

tion; it is about the struggle for truth when you feel you have truly been victimized. It is both philosophical and poetic and should be read because it is written in response to the age-old question: why do the righteous suffer?

Do you know a story of suffering you want to share? Either write it down or discuss it on our blog in this context.

Day Eleven

Begin the day by making a wish for someone else, just after waking. Get comfortable in your wishing/meditation space. Sit up with your eyes closed and your palms on top of your thighs. Take a deep breath in through your nose and exhale out through your mouth, and repeat. Continue focusing on your breathing throughout the whole process of making a wish. Breathe in: I believe therefore I accept. Breathe out: I am a believer therefore my wish has already come true. Breathe in: Say the wish for someone else. Breathe out: See it in your mind and feel it; smile while feeling the wish is becoming real. It is crystal clear what you are wishing for and you can experience the emotion of happiness while watching your wish come true in your mind.

Your last wish of the day, before bed, and to end this course is this: Close your eyes as always and make a wish for all your wishes to come true plus your daily wish. Like the classic "wishing for more wishes" you are doing something similar. Make a wish for your wishes to come true and for unexpected and wonderful things to continue to happen in your life. Take a deep breath in through your nose and exhale out through your mouth, and do this twice. Continue focusing on your breathing throughout the whole process of making a wish. Breathe in: I believe therefore I accept. Breathe out: I am a believer therefore my wish has already come true. Breathe in: Say your wish and wish for all your wishes to come true. Breathe out: See it in your mind and feel it; smile while feeling the wish is becoming real. It is crystal clear what you are wishing for and you can experience the emotion of happiness while watching your wish come true in your mind.

For this day, we are looking at the new book *Give and Take: A Revolutionary Approach to Success*, by Adam Grant.

In this popular book he discusses his research and examines the surprising forces that shape why some people rise to the top of the success ladder while others stay at the bottom. In professional interactions, it turns out most people operate as *takers, matchers,* or *givers*. Takers strive to get as much as possible from others, whereas matchers aim to trade evenly. Givers are the rare breed of people who contribute to others without expecting anything in return. The givers are the most successful people in his analysis.

After reading that book, or at least the first chapter, write down your thoughts on a pad or on our blog. This is the beginning of a new paradigm for you, perhaps. As a wish maker, a miracle worker, or whatever you want to call it, you have a new practice, a new yoga of wishing that requires a small amount of time, and actions with which you choose to support your wishes. Those actions might come from one of the books you have just read or the exercises we wrote down. Perhaps like Adam Grant suggests, you will be a conscious giver.

Conclusion—The Wishing Life

One more method to consider is a simple one we use. It works like this. Choose something that makes you happy in a comforting and even materialistic way that you could do every day. It could be the process of petting your dog or cat, or maybe trying on a different make-up every day, or reading a mystery book. Something simple that does not seem profound, but that has personal meaning to you. We each use our own. Delia likes to use make-up applications as her daily meditation; that is, a set of actions with no meaning other than the intrinsic happiness it brings her. Brainard likes to pet his dog every day for his action that makes him happy. As we both do these actions every day, we do them consciously, knowing that we are creating a small amount of euphoria for ourselves in a simple way. Here is the catch. Do this every day for thirty days if possible, for the pure pleasure of it. But after you spend five or ten minutes on this activity, whatever it is, close your eyes and make a wish of some kind. Wish for anything you like, but wish. The reason for doing so is that you are consciously creating a moment of happiness for yourself. In that moment you can make a wish and it will mean something to you. It also associates wish making with happiness and that is how it should be.

Though this is a very simple exercise, it can have profound effects if you practice it regularly as a way to induce peace of mind and encourage wishes.

Last Note on Wishing Practice

This is a book on wishing, and it is meant to inspire your practice and to be a course to build a path to a better understanding of what it means to make wishes come true, or at least to give them the best chance of becoming real.

The practice of wishing is one of community, because to wish for others is of great benefit to us all. The altruistic gesture is one that we believe is rewarded on many personal levels. We have set up a blog to discuss the wishes and practice you are doing, at www.schoolofwishing.com, but it is also a place for like-minded individuals to share thoughts so that the community of wishers will grow and hopefully change the world for the better. Join us and tell us your wish. Become a teacher of wishing. When you have completed the reading and course assignments, or as much of them as you can, tell us on the blog and we will send you your wishing diploma!

The End

www.schoolofwishing.com